CAMPAIGN • 256

FALLEN TIMBERS

The US Army's first victory

JOHN F WINKLER

ILLUSTRATED BY PETER DENNIS

Series editor Marcus Cowper

First published in Great Britain in 2013 by Osprey Publishing,
PO Box 883, Oxford, OX1 9PL, UK
PO Box 3985, New York, NY 10185-3985, USA
Email: info@ospreypublishing.com

Osprey Publishing is part of the Osprey Group.

A CIP catalog record for this book is available from the British Library.

ISBN: 978 1 78096 375 4
Ebook ISBN: 978 1 78096 376 1
Epub ISBN: 978 1 78096 377 8

Editorial by Ilios Publishing Ltd, Oxford, UK (www.iliospublishing.com)
Index by Alan Thatcher
Maps by Bounford.com
3D bird's-eye view by The Black Spot
Battlescene illustrations by Peter Dennis
Typeset in Myriad Pro and Sabon
Originated by PDQ Media, Bungay, UK
Printed in China through World Print Ltd.

14 15 16 17 18   11 10 9 8 7 6 5 4 3 2

www.ospreypublishing.com

AUTHOR'S NOTE

Beckie Finch of Metroparks of the Toledo Area, Dave Westrick of the Fallen
Timbers Battlefield Association, Clay Johnson of the Garst Museum, Nancy
Meiring Knapke and Christine Keller of the Fort Recovery State Museum,
Le Ann Hendershott of the Campus Martius Museum of the Northwest
Territory, and John MacLeod of Fort Malden National Historic Site of
Canada offered valuable assistance in assembling materials for this book.
Dale Benington and John Stanton generously provided illustrations from
their extensive collections of site photographs. Sonja Cropper, Robert Hart,
Jonathan Winkler, and Wendy S. Winkler were kind enough to find or take
other site photographs.

ARTIST'S NOTE

Readers may care to note that the original paintings from which the color
plates in this book were prepared are available for private sale.
The Publishers retain all reproduction copyright whatsoever.
All enquiries should be addressed to:

Peter Dennis, Fieldhead, The Park, Mansfield, NOTTS, NG18 2AT, UK

Email: magieh@ntlworld.com

The Publishers regret that they can enter into no correspondence upon
this matter.

THE WOODLAND TRUST

Osprey Publishing are supporting the Woodland Trust, the UK's leading
woodland conservation charity, by funding the dedication of trees.

Key to military symbols

xxxxx	xxxx	xxx	xx	x	III	II
Army Group	Army	Corps	Division	Brigade	Regiment	Battalion
Company/Battery	Platoon	Section	Squad	Infantry	Artillery	Cavalry
Airborne	Unit HQ	Air defense	Air Force	Air mobile	Air transportable	Amphibious
Antitank	Armor	Air aviation	Bridging	Engineer	Headquarters	Maintenance
Medical	Missile	Mountain	Navy	Nuclear, biological, chemical	Ordnance	Parachute
Reconnaissance	Signal	Supply	Transport movement	Rocket artillery	Air defense artillery	

Key to unit identification

Unit identifier — Parent unit — Commander
(+) with added elements
(−) less elements

CONTENTS

The situation in eastern North America in 1792

Lake Superior

BRITISH UPPER CANADA

BRITISH LOWER CANADA

DISPUTED BRITISH AND AMERICAN

Quebec

Ottawa River

Montreal

St. Lawrence River

MASSACHUSETTS

VERMONT

Fort Mackinac

Lake Huron

NEW HAMPSHIRE

Toronto (1793)

Lake Ontario

Lake Michigan

Newark

Fort Niagara

NEW YORK

MASSACHUSETTS

Boston

Fort Detroit

Lake Erie

Allegheny River

CONNECTICUT

RHODE ISLAND

NORTHWEST TERRITORY OF THE UNITED STATES

Fallen Timbers (Aug. 20, 1794)

Maumee River

Wabash River

Fort Franklin

Wabash (Nov. 4, 1791)

PENNSYLVANIA

New York

Fort Fayette (Pittsburgh)

Philadelphia

NEW JERSEY

Fort Jefferson

Fort Hamilton

Fort Harmar

Ohio River

MARYLAND

DELAWARE

St. Louis

Fort Knox (Vincennes)

Fort Washington (Cincinnati)

Fort Steuben

Alexandria

Fort Massac (1794)

Lexington

KENTUCKY

VIRGINIA

Richmond

SPANISH LOUISIANA

SOUTHWEST TERRITORY OF THE UNITED STATES

NORTH CAROLINA

Mississippi River

GEORGIA

SOUTH CAROLINA

Charleston

SPANISH WEST FLORIDA

Savannah

ATLANTIC OCEAN

New Orleans

St Augustine

GULF OF MEXICO

SPANISH EAST FLORIDA

N

- ■ US Army forts
- ☐ British forts on American territory
- ● Cities and towns
- ✕ Battlefields
- ★ Future sites
- British territory
- Spanish territory
- Disputed territory
- US national territory
- US state territory

0   200 miles

0   200km

INTRODUCTION

After the Ohio Indians destroyed the US Army at the battle of the Wabash in 1791, President George Washington recalled Maj. Gen. Anthony Wayne from retirement to lead a new army against them. As Wayne trained his soldiers and devised new tactics and weapons to use against the Indians, the obstacles he faced multiplied. Ahead of him, British and Spanish armies seemed likely to join the Indians. Behind him, a French army of American volunteers in Kentucky and a rebel force in western Pennsylvania threatened to cut his army off from the United States. Within his ranks, a treasonous conspiracy led by his principal subordinate endangered his command and his life.

Wayne at last led his new US Army against the Ohio Indians, who for 40 years had defeated British and American armies sent against them. Deep in the Ohio wilderness, they awaited the Americans at Fallen Timbers. There, on August 20, 1794, Wayne led the US Army to the first victory in its history and secured for the United States a future west of the Appalachian Mountains.

THE STRATEGIC SITUATION

The Ohio River frontier

In 1792, the first term of the first president of the United States, George Washington, was approaching its end. Nine years before Britain had recognized American independence in the Treaty of Paris. Four years before, the 13 American states had created a federal government by adopting the US Constitution. In 1791 and 1792, two new states, Vermont and Kentucky, had joined the original 13.

LEFT
The Ohio River today, as seen from Marietta, Ohio. (Photograph by Wendy S. Winkler)

RIGHT
This reconstructed British trading post and stockade is at the site of Peckuwe, now George Rogers Clark Memorial Park near Springfield, Ohio. (Author's photograph)

About 4,000,000 Americans lived within the boundary of the United States that had been established in the Treaty of Paris. In addition to the states, American territory included two federal territories. The Southwest Territory would become the state of Tennessee. The Northwest Territory lay between the Ohio River, the Mississippi River, and the Great Lakes.

Almost 30 years before, Americans had begun settling in the endless forests that lay between the Appalachian Mountains and the Ohio River. By 1792, about 175,000 lived on the Ohio River frontier. Their largest urban centers: Pittsburgh in Pennsylvania and Lexington, Washington, and Louisville in Kentucky had populations of only a few hundred.

Most Americans on the frontier lived on scattered homesteads, often many miles from their nearest neighbors. Hundreds of miles of rough roads or horse trails through the mountains lay between them and the remainder of the American population. From Philadelphia, the American federal capital, a journey to the frontier was longer than one to London or Paris.

For almost 20 years, the Americans on the frontier had been at war with the Ohio Indians. The fighting, which had commenced in 1774 in Lord Dunmore's War, had continued into the Revolutionary War, in which most of the Ohio Indians had fought as British allies. During the Revolutionary War, American militia forces led by Brig. Gen. George Rogers Clark had captured Vincennes in 1779, defeated the Ohio Indians at Peckuwe in 1780, and driven the Indians from southern Ohio in 1782. Because of Clark's victories, the Treaty of Paris had given the United States western boundaries defined by the Great Lakes and the Mississippi River.

After the Revolutionary War, Virginia had granted to the United States the area that would be named the Northwest Territory. There, the federal government had expected to compensate Revolutionary War veterans with land grants and to generate from land sales profits that would reduce the national debt. By 1792, however, only about 3,000 settlers had moved into the territory. The main urban center, three-year-old Cincinnati, had a population of about 400. Other centers included Marietta, founded in 1788; Gallipolis, settled in 1790; and Vincennes, an older French settlement that was becoming American.

Continuing raids by the Ohio Indians had discouraged settlement beyond the Ohio. The Treaties of Fort Stanwix in 1784, Fort Macintosh in 1785, Fort Finney in 1786, and Fort Harmar in 1789 all had failed to produce peace on the frontier. Military operations had also proved fruitless. In 1786, Clark had assembled an army of 3,000 Kentuckians to end permanently the raiding of the Ohio Indians. A mysterious mutiny, however, had terminated his campaign and his military career. Subsequent campaigns by other Kentucky leaders had failed to stop Indian raids.

In 1790, President Washington had decided to use the US Army to suppress the Ohio Indians. Created in 1784, this American federal army had replaced the Continental Army Washington had led during the Revolutionary War. A 1790 US Army campaign by Brig. Gen. Josiah Harmar had failed. A 1791 campaign by Maj. Gen. Arthur St. Clair had ended in disaster. On November 4, 1791, the Ohio Indians had destroyed most of the US Army at the battle of the Wabash.

In 1792, what remained of the US Army garrisoned eight forts on the frontier. Between Fort Franklin on the Allegheny River and Fort Knox on the Wabash River, Forts Fayette, Harmar, Washington, and Steuben guarded the 705-mile long Ohio River frontier from Pittsburgh to Louisville. Fort Hamilton and Fort Jefferson, built beyond the Ohio River during St. Clair's campaign, were the army's most advanced outposts. State militia forts, such as Fort Randolph at the mouth of the Kanawha River and Scott's Blockhouse at the mouth of the Kentucky, defended critical geographical positions. Small settlers' fortresses, usually called forts or stations, served as refuges from Indian attacks.

The Indians who had defeated St. Clair were drawn from a population of perhaps 15,000, who lived in what is now Ohio, Indiana, southern Michigan, and southwestern Ontario. Like the Americans, the Indians had arrived in the area during the 18th century. For decades before 1701, war between the Iroquois of upstate New York, a confederacy of the Mohawk, Oneida, Onondaga, Cayuga, and Seneca tribes, and Indians as far west as the Mississippi River had made the area too dangerous for habitation.

This portrait by an unknown artist depicts Sir Guy Carleton, Baron Dorchester. (Courtesy of Library and Archives Canada, C-002833)

During the subsequent repopulation of the area, interactions among members of formerly hostile Indian tribes, and with French, British, and American traders, settlers, and adopted captives, left many individuals difficult to categorize. By 1792, almost a century of life in the area had blurred genetic distinctions and cultural identities. Most of the Ohio Indians were, by traditional rules of patrilineal and matrilineal descent or by adoption, members of the Delaware, Miami, Mingo, Ojibwe, Ottawa, Potawatomi, Shawnee, or Wyandot tribes, and of subgroups within the tribes. They varied, however, in the extent to which they followed traditional patterns of Indian life.

Most Indians lived at least part of the year in villages in which one tribe predominated. Because the Ohio Indian tribes seldom claimed exclusive settlement areas, villages of different tribes were often concentrated in close proximity. Around them spread fields and orchards, where women, children, and slaves labored. From the villages, trails led south through tens of thousands of square miles of uninhabited forest, where Indian men hunted, to American settlements, where they raided.

To the north and northeast lay British Canada. In 1791, Britain had reorganized its largest North American colony, Quebec, into two provinces, Lower and Upper Canada. Sir Guy Carleton, Baron Dorchester, the governor of Canada, ruled both. The commander of British forces in North America at the end of the Revolutionary War, he had supervised the evacuation of the last British units and the relocation of loyalist refugees to Canada. The United States, Dorchester believed, was too unstable to survive for long.

By 1792, the British had secured by Indian treaties almost all of the land on the northern shores of Lake Ontario and Lake Erie. There, in Upper Canada, about 15,000 settlers, many loyalist refugees, lived in homesteads much like those of the Americans. The province had two urban centers in the primary areas of settlement. Newark, now Niagara-on-the Lake, Ontario, served as the capital of Upper Canada. Far to the west, in an area of about 4,000 settlers, rapidly growing Detroit had a population of more than 1,500.

Three British forts protected the areas where population was greatest: Forts Niagara and Erie, garrisoned by the British 5th Regiment of Foot, guarded the area near Newark. At Fort Lernoult, usually called Fort Detroit, the 24th Regiment of Foot defended the area around Detroit.

The forts and settlements of Upper Canada, unlike those of the Americans to the south, could be reached by water routes from the Atlantic Ocean. From Montreal, watercraft could travel as far as Newark and Fort Niagara. After a short portage around the Niagara Falls, soldiers, settlers, and supplies could move by ship on the Niagara River and Lake Erie.

The photograph, taken from the site of Navy Hall, shows Fort Niagara in the distance, just to the right of the mouth of the Niagara River on Lake Ontario. (Photograph by Dale Benington)

From Navy Hall, the capitol of Upper Canada in Newark, Lt. Col. John Graves Simcoe ruled the province as Dorchester's lieutenant governor. Simcoe had served during the Revolutionary War as commander of the Queen's Rangers, a loyalist irregular unit. Like Dorchester, he believed that a renewal of the Revolutionary War was inevitable.

Both the British and the Americans had grounds for commencing hostilities. The insolvent US government had failed to pay amounts owed to Britain under the Treaty of Paris. The British had failed to surrender land due the United States under the treaty. British Fort Niagara, Fort Detroit, and Fort Mackinac in northern Michigan, all lay within American territory.

The Legion of the United States

On March 5, 1792, Congress created a new US Army, which would be called the Legion of the United States. To command its more than 5,000 officers and men, Washington considered many prominent Revolutionary War officers, three of whom lived on the Ohio River frontier.

The first, Lt. Col. James Wilkinson, was a Pennsylvanian who had moved to Kentucky in 1784. In 1786, he had founded Frankfort, which would become the state capital in 1792. In 1787, he had won wide popularity in Kentucky by traveling to New Orleans and persuading the Spanish to open the Mississippi River briefly to American commerce. In 1791, he had secured for himself an appointment as commander of the US 2nd Infantry Regiment.

The second, Maj. Gen. Charles Scott, had served as Washington's chief of intelligence. A Virginian, he had moved to Kentucky in 1787. After losing two sons in Indian raids, he had by 1792 become a leading Kentucky militia leader.

The third, Brig. Gen. Rufus Putnam, had commanded two Massachusetts regiments at Saratoga and served as Washington's principal engineer. In 1788, he had organized a company of prominent New England Revolutionary War officers to purchase land in the Northwest Territory. In 1792, he led the settlers to the Northwest Territory's first American settlement, Marietta.

St. Clair's resignation left Wilkinson as the highest-ranking officer in the US Army. The ambitious Wilkinson used what remained of the army to defend the most advanced American forts. In January 1792 he led a relief convoy to Fort Jefferson. On February 1 he briefly returned with a party to the site of the battle of the Wabash. He then built a new fort halfway between Fort Hamilton and Fort Jefferson, which he named Fort St. Clair. Wilkinson's US Army soldiers, however, could do little beyond defend their forts. On February 11, the commandant of Fort Jefferson lost a son when he dared to go hunting in the nearby woods. On April 27, Indians killed his successor.

Beyond the walls of the forts, war raged between the Indians and settlers. On March 15, Indians killed three at Newbury, a settlement near Marietta that then was abandoned. At about the same time, 100 Shawnee led by Black Hoof battled 37 Kentuckians led by the famous frontiersman Simon Kenton at Salt Lick. Three Indians and two of Kenton's men fell before the Kentuckians fled.

To his bitter disappointment, Wilkinson did not receive his expected appointment as commander of the Legion, but only a promotion to brigadier-general. Washington instead chose Maj. Gen. Anthony Wayne to lead the Legion. After assuming command on April 13, Wayne went west to Fort Fayette, recently built to replace the decayed Fort Pitt. There he planned to train his arriving soldiers before commencing a campaign in Ohio in 1793.

When Wayne reached Fort Fayette on June 14, he first addressed the situation on the frontier. On May 22, Indians had killed or captured 11 settlers near Reed's Station on the Allegheny River. On May 23, they had killed two and captured two others near Fort Randolph. In May and June, they had killed or captured several men near Marietta.

Wayne dispatched soldiers to garrison a series of new US Army strongholds to protect the settlers. On the Allegheny, Wayne sent men to Mead's Station, Kittanning, and Reed's Station. On the Ohio, soldiers arrived at Beaver Blockhouse, Mingo Bottom, Wheeling, and Gallipolis.

Wayne also sought advice from two famous frontiersman: William McMahon and Samuel Brady. McMahon had accepted a commission as a major in the Legion. Brady, after serving with Wayne during the Revolutionary War, had become a legendary figure fighting Indians on the Ohio frontier. About to be tortured to death in 1780, he had escaped. Pursued by hundreds of Indians, he then had avoided recapture by "Brady's Leap," a prodigious, 25ft vault across a gorge in what is now Kent, Ohio.

McMahon and Brady recommended recruiting a corps of experienced scouts to patrol the woods along the frontier. Brady agreed to lead a company on the upper Ohio River. The famous frontiersmen Samuel Davis and Cornelius Washburn joined the scouts who would guard the area from Cincinnati to Washington, Kentucky.

As Wayne organized the defense of the frontier, others who had received commissions spread out across the United States to recruit soldiers. Many of the best American officers of the Revolutionary War had fallen at Wabash,

including Wayne's friend Maj. Gen. Richard Butler. But distinguished veterans like Putnam, and Wayne's close friend Brig. Gen. Thomas Posey, left retirement to join the survivors.

Promising younger men also came forward: 28-year-old Capt. William Eaton recruited a company of "Green Mountain Boys" for the army in the new state of Vermont; 22-year-old William Clark, a younger brother of George Rogers Clark, received a commission as lieutenant; 24-year-old Hugh Brady, younger brother of Samuel Brady, became an ensign.

The Americans, however, hoped to end the frontier violence without another campaign. Washington asked the Mohawk leader Joseph Brant, who had led the anti-American Iroquois during the Revolutionary War, to come to Philadelphia. Brant, a Freemason who had translated the Gospel of Mark into Mohawk, agreed to convey to the Indians the American peace proposals. Colonel John Hardin, a leading Kentucky militia leader, volunteered to travel under a white flag to Indian villages on the Sandusky River. US Army Capt. Alexander Truman, after recovering from wounds suffered at Wabash, agreed to go to villages on the Maumee.

In June, Kentuckians and Indians met at a prisoner exchange arranged by French settlers at Vincennes. The adopted Miami William Wells, who had led an Indian unit at Wabash, attended to secure the release of his wife, the daughter of the Miami commander Little Turtle. There he met his brother, Capt. Samuel Wells, a survivor of Wabash, who persuaded him to return to Kentucky.

Some of the Indians at the prisoner exchange agreed to attend a peace council in Vincennes in September. Putnam, who offered to serve as the American negotiator, sought from Philadelphia instructions on acceptable peace terms. Wells agreed to serve as Putnam's interpreter.

Through the summer of 1792, however, war continued on the frontier. On June 25, 15 soldiers ventured from Fort Jefferson to gather food for horses. At what would be remembered as the Haycutters Massacre, 50 Indians killed or captured them all. At about the same time, Scott led almost 1,000 Kentucky horsemen across the Ohio. Reaching the Eel River undetected, they attacked Miami villages, where they killed several Indians and captured more than 20.

Across the frontier, Indian raiders attacked American settlements in July and August. Near Cincinnati and Gallipolis, Dunlap's Station, Covalt's Station, and Washington, Kentucky, they killed and scalped. At isolated cabins even American children fought for their lives. When a Shawnee badly wounded the only adult male at Stevenson's Station in Kentucky, eight-year-old Andrew Stevenson saved his family by killing the Indian with a small hunting gun.

Fear spread even to Fort Fayette. On August 8, the guards at Wayne's outposts fled from approaching Indians in panic. When his scouts reported that there had been only six Indians, the American commander realized that a new training program was needed. Soon his soldiers were fighting mock battles against frontiersmen dressed as Indian warriors, who attacked them using Indian tactics.

The attempts to negotiate a peace failed. Hardin and Truman were killed and scalped. Putnam's council in Vincennes ended on September 24 with a vague agreement that there should be peace. Fourteen of the Indians who attended then left to continue raiding in Kentucky. On September 29, 20 others killed two soldiers near Fort Jefferson.

This photograph, taken about 1850, shows Samuel Brady's brother, Hugh Brady. A lieutenant in Preston's rifle company at Fallen Timbers, Hugh Brady would end his US Army career as a major-general. (Library of Congress, Prints and Photographs Division)

In October thousands of Indians gathered at the mouth of the Auglaize River on the Maumee at a site known as the Glaize. Three who attended, Americans who had fought with the Ohio Indians during the Revolutionary War, were especially vocal in urging the Indians not to allow settlement beyond the Ohio River. Alexander McKee, whom Wayne would call "the chief instigator" of war on the Ohio River frontier, had arrived from his trading post at the foot of the Maumee Rapids. McKee, who had a Shawnee mother and adopted Shawnee father, was the chief British Indian agent. Matthew Elliott, a Detroit trader with a Shawnee wife, served as McKee's assistant. With them was the adopted Mingo Simon Girty, who had led an Indian unit at Wabash.

A consensus soon emerged. The Indians would assemble for a council at Sandusky the following June. If the Americans wanted peace, they could send emissaries to Sandusky to acknowledge that the Ohio River would be the boundary of American settlement.

Little Turtle then led 300 warriors south to raid. After killing three settlers near Washington, Kentucky, and another near Covalt's Station, they learned from four soldiers taken near Fort Hamilton that a large packhorse convoy was on its way back from Fort Jefferson. On November 5, they found it, camped 200yds from Fort St. Clair.

Just before dawn on November 6, the Indians attacked. Major John Adair, who would later be a Kentucky senator and governor, and Lt. George Madison, a Wabash survivor who also would be a Kentucky governor, led the 120 Kentucky mounted riflemen who served as convoy guards. As the fort's small US Army garrison watched, the Indians battled the Kentucky horsemen for about 30 minutes. Before the Indians withdrew, they killed six and wounded 20 of the Kentuckians.

Adair's men, who claimed the battlefield, considered the battle of Fort St. Clair a victory. Little Turtle, however, had accomplished his purpose. The Indians had taken 160 packhorses. Until new ones were obtained, there would be no more supply convoys to Fort Jefferson.

Wayne, however, had been busy at Fort Fayette. As Adair's Kentuckians were fighting, flatboats were arriving at Fort Washington with the first reinforcements from the new American army. Wilkinson now would have three dragoon troops and two rifle companies from the Legion to protect convoys.

This portrait by Nicola Marschall depicts John Adair. In 1815 Adair would lead the Kentucky riflemen who fought at the battle of New Orleans. (Courtesy of the Kentucky Historical Society)

On November 8, Wayne dispatched McMahon and 64 frontiersmen on a long-range scouting expedition. From Mingo Bottom they went deep into Ohio searching for Indians. After killing two and wounding a third, they returned without suffering any casualties.

On November 18, Wayne moved his army 22 miles down the Ohio to a winter camp, which he named Legion Ville. At the camp, now usually called Legionville, he learned of the Indian invitation to send peace commissioners to the council at Sandusky. "I have a strong propensity to attend," Wayne wrote to Secretary of War Henry Knox, "with about 2,500 commissioners … among whom I do not wish to have a single Quaker."

As Wayne planned his 1793 campaign, Indian raiding continued. In December, Shawnees besieged Big Sandy Station, killed a man near from Massie's Station and captured Samuel Davis, who soon escaped. On April 1, 1793, 30 Shawnee and Chickamauga Cherokee from Paint Creek attacked Morgan's Station in Kentucky, killing, capturing, or wounding 20. Kenton, Washburn, and 30 Kentuckians then attacked the Indians at Reeves Corssing on Paint Creek. There they killed the Indians' leader, John Ward, the brother of a Washington settler, and three warriors.

East of the Appalachians, however, the patriotic fervor that had followed Wabash had waned. Because of political pressure, Knox wrote to Wayne on April 13, the government would send peace commissioners to Sandusky. "Their lives," he added, "will depend upon an absolute restraining of all hostile or offensive operations."

Wayne, who feared that the government might succumb to pressure to agree to the Indians' demands, responded that such action would endanger the future of the United States. "Should the Ohio eventually be made the boundary," he warned, "the United States will soon experience a formidable neighbor upon its margin, who will immediately open a wide and deep drain to the population of the Atlantic states." On April 20, Knox sent Wayne instructions to proceed to Fort Washington. There he would receive a letter directly from the commissioners. If it contained a prearranged, apparently innocuous, sentence, the American commander was to commence operations against the Indians.

The six Kentuckians killed at Fort St. Clair were buried beside this oak, which survives at Fort St. Clair State Park near Eaton, Ohio. (Photograph by John Stanton)

The site of Legionville today. (Author's collection)

During the year since Wayne's appointment, however, events had greatly complicated the situation in which such operations would occur. In 1778, when the government of King Louis XVI had agreed to support the Americans in the Revolutionary War, the United States had entered into a treaty of alliance with France. On January 21, 1793, however, a revolutionary government had publicly executed the French king. On February 1, 1793, the new French government had declared war on Britain and, on March 7, on Spain.

The British and Spanish, who believed that the United States would honor its treaty with France, began preparing for war in North America. Simcoe, who had concluded that his capital was too near the American border, had prepared a new site, to be called York, and later Toronto. He had begun recruiting as allies against the Americans the Iroquois of Upper Canada and New York. At the same time, the Spanish in New Orleans had sent emissaries to potential allies: the Cherokees, Creeks, Choctaws, and Chickasaws of Spanish West Florida and Louisiana, Georgia, and the Southwest Territory.

On April 8, a minister from the new French government had arrived in the United States. Edmond-Charles Genêt, who saw himself as a leader of an international revolutionary movement rather than a national emissary, was eager to begin managing the American theater of war. Instead of presenting himself at Philadelphia, he had sailed to Charleston to recruit ships and crews for a naval campaign in the British West Indies.

Genêt had ambitious plans. He would have an American army invade Spanish East and West Florida and add the areas to the United States. Other American armies would invade British Canada, and Spanish Louisiana and Mexico. There, revolutionary movements would establish independent states allied with France.

This 1897 Howard Pyle engraving depicts Washington's reception of Genêt in 1793. When the French minister's replacement arrived in 1794 with a warrant for his arrest, Washington, who referred to Genêt in private correspondence as "that thing," granted him asylum in the United States. (Courtesy of Harper's Magazine)

This 1813 portrait by John Wesley Jarvis depicts Brig. Gen. James Wilkinson, whom Wayne would call "the worst of all bad men." (Courtesy of the Filson Historical Society, Louisville, Ky.)

Welcomed everywhere by local officials and enthusiastic crowds, Genêt then had traveled to the American capital. There, however, he had received bad news. Because Britain and Spain had not attacked France, Washington announced on April 23 that the United States would remain neutral.

Genêt then made new plans. He would recruit for his North American armies American volunteers, who, if necessary, would renounce their citizenship and become French soldiers. He also would take action to replace the American government in Philadelphia with one more sympathetic to the ideals of the French Revolution.

West of the Appalachians, dissatisfaction with the American federal government had become widespread. Its US Army soldiers had begun to resemble a foreign army of occupation, sent from Philadelphia to control the western settlements. On February 12, 1792, an officer sued by a Cincinnati man had sent a sergeant and 20 soldiers to attack the man's lawyer. A mob of settlers then had driven the soldiers back to Fort Washington. To pay for St. Clair's campaign, moreover, the federal government had imposed a tax on distillers that had proven uncollectable in the west. On September 15, 1792, the federal government had announced that revenue officers led by Brig. Gen. John Neville would begin enforcing it in western Pennsylvania.

Events in Kentucky had created other dangers that would imperil Wayne's campaign. George Rogers Clark had ended his military career with vast tracts of land in Kentucky. In November 1792, however, a Kentucky court had impoverished him by ruling that others owned the property he claimed. "My country," Clark wrote to Genêt, "has proved notoriously ungrateful for my services … which gave it the whole of its territory on this side of the great mountains." He was willing, he said, to lead an army of American volunteers in a French campaign to conquer Spanish Louisiana.

As Wilkinson awaited the arrival of his commander, he was receiving secret shipments of gold from Spanish Louisiana. After arriving in the west with dreams of obtaining unrivaled power beyond the Appalachians, he had agreed to become a Spanish agent. He first had worked to create an independent Kentucky, which would enter into an alliance with Spain. When that effort failed, he had used his powerful political connections to secure his high command in the US Army. Expecting imminent war with the United States, the Spanish now wanted him to take action to ensure that Wayne's army would pose no threat in the coming hostilities.

Wilkinson was prepared to undertake such a mission. When he had arrived in Kentucky, he had found in Clark a formidable obstacle to achieving his goal of ruling an empire west of the Appalachians. The mutiny that had ended Clark's 1786 campaign had been his work, achieved by a covert campaign of manipulating disloyal officers, spreading false rumors, and denying supplies needed by Clark's army. When Wayne arrived at Fort Washington to commence his campaign, another campaign, led by Wilkinson, also would begin.

CHRONOLOGY

*c.*1640–1701	Beaver Wars depopulate Ohio River frontier area.
1701–73	Repopulation of Ohio River frontier area.
1774	Lord Dunmore's War.
1775–82	Revolutionary War.
January 14, 1784	Congress agrees to Treaty of Paris.
January 1, 1785	Treaty of Fort Mcintosh.
January 31, 1786	Treaty of Fort Finney.
July 12, 1787	Congress enacts Northwest Ordinance, creating the Northwest Territory.
June 21, 1788	Vote of New Hampshire to ratify US Constitution creates permanent federal government for United States.
January 9, 1789	Treaty of Fort Harmar.
April 30, 1789	Washington inaugurated as president.
September 26– November 3, 1790	Harmar's campaign.
November 4, 1791	Battle of the Wabash.

1792

April 13	Anthony Wayne assumes command of Legion of the United States.
June 25	Haycutters Massacre.
November 6	Battle of Fort St. Clair.

1793

April 8	Genêt arrives in Charleston.
May 5	Legion reaches first camp (Hobson's Choice).
September 11	Wayne receives coded message authorizing commencement of campaign.

October 7	Legion reaches second camp.
October 8	Legion reaches third camp.
October 9	Legion reaches fourth camp.
October 10	Legion reaches fifth camp.
October 11	Legion reaches sixth camp.
October 12	Legion reaches seventh camp.
October 13	Legion reaches eighth camp.
October 17	Battle of Lowry Run.
November 6	Americans begin building Fort Greeneville.
December 25	Americans begin building Fort Recovery.

1794

January 1	Collins's Fight.
March 24	Washington Proclamation ends George Rogers Clark Expedition Against Spanish Louisiana.
April 10	British begin building Fort Miamis.
May 13	Clark's Ambush.
June 12	Americans begin building Fort Massac.
June 30–July 1	Battle of Fort Recovery.
July 16	Attack on Neville House begins Whiskey Rebellion.
July 28	Legion advances to ninth camp.
July 29	Legion advances to tenth camp.
July 30	Legion advances to 11th camp.
August 1	Legion advances to 12th camp; begins building Fort Adams.
August 3	Tree falls on Wayne's tent. Barbee's Brigade joins the Legion.
August 4	Legion advances to 13th camp.
August 5	Legion advances to 14th camp.
August 6	Legion advances to 15th camp.
August 7	Legion advances to 16th camp. Washington issues Whiskey Rebellion Proclamation.
August 8	Legion advances to 17th camp; begins building Fort Defiance.
August 15	Legion advances to 18th camp.
August 16	Legion advances to 19th camp.
August 17	Legion advances to 20th camp.
August 18	Legion advances to 21st camp; begins building Fort Deposit.
August 20	Battle of Fallen Timbers; Legion advances to 22nd camp.
August 22	Wayne examines Fort Miamis.

August 23	Legion returns to 21st camp.
August 24	Legion returns to 20th camp.
August 25	Legion reaches 23rd camp.
August 26	Legion returns to 18th camp.
August 27	Legion reaches 24th camp.
September 14	Legion reaches 25th camp.
September 15	Legion reaches 26th camp.
September 16	Legion reaches 27th camp.
September 17	Legion reaches 28th camp; begins building Fort Wayne.
October 27	Legion reaches 29th camp.
October 28	Legion reaches 30th camp.
October 29	Legion reaches 31st camp.
October 30	Legion reaches 32nd camp.
November 1	Legion reaches 33rd camp. Federal Army enters western Pennsylvania to suppress Whiskey Rebellion.
November 2	Legion reaches Fort Greeneville.

1795

August 3	Treaty of Greeneville ends Indian war.

OPPOSING COMMANDERS

AMERICAN

Major-General Anthony Wayne, the commanding general of the US Army, led the campaign. Although he would be remembered as "Mad" Anthony Wayne, an epithet received from a Revolutionary War soldier denied a request, he was a very careful commander. The Indians called him "Blacksnake" because such creatures, they believed, never slept. They thought, wrote the Shawnee Jonathan Alder, "he was always awake and you could never take him by surprise. They supposed him to be something supernatural."

Wayne first won fame for his capture of Stony Point in 1779. Two later experiences during the Revolutionary War prepared him for what he would face on the Ohio River frontier, a conspiracy within his army and battle with Indians. On January 1, 1781, the 2,400 men in Wayne's Pennsylvania regiments mutinied. Despite British attempts to persuade his soldiers to defect, he successfully satisfied their grievances and ended the crisis. On June 24, 1782, while Wayne was besieging Savannah, Creek Indians attacked his camp at night. At the battle of Ebenezer Creek, his men drove the Creeks from the camp with bayonets and killed their leader, the famous chief Emistisiguo.

This portrait by James Sharples, Sr. depicts Maj. Gen. Anthony Wayne a few months before his death in 1796. (Independence National Historical Park)

At Fallen Timbers, Wayne's army consisted of US Army soldiers, nominally organized into four sublegions of the Legion of the United States, and volunteer Kentucky horsemen. Wayne's two principal US Army subordinates were **Brig. Gen. James Wilkinson** and **Lt. Col. John Hamtramck**, a French Canadian who had fought with the Americans during the Revolutionary War. Wilkinson nominally led the army's "Right Wing," which contained the 1st and 3rd Sublegions, and Hamtramck the "Left Wing," which contained the 2nd and 4th.

Wayne's actual delegations of command at Fallen Timbers, however, addressed an unusual problem. Wayne knew that Wilkinson was capable of treachery. He also was uncertain whether he could trust Hamtramck.

Although Wayne left Wilkinson and Hamtramck in command of the Wings, he detached about half of the sublegions' units to a "Center and Reserve" under his personal command. At the battle, he also sent orders directly to the commanders of the units left in Wilkinson and Hamtramck's wings.

Wayne's staff included his Adjutant General, Maj. John Mills, his Quartermaster General, James O'Hara, and his aides de camp, Capt. Henry De Butts, Capt. Thomas Lewis, and Lt. William Henry Harrison. The prodigious logistical efforts of O'Hara, a Pittsburgh trader, enabled Wayne's army to reach Fallen Timbers. O'Hara's principal subordinate, Deputy Quartermaster General Maj. John Belli, led Wayne's intelligence network of buyers and suppliers. De Butts had survived the battle of the Wabash. Harrison would defeat the Indians at the battle of Tippecanoe in 1811, prevail over the British at the battle of the Thames in 1813, and be elected the ninth president of the United States in 1840.

Wayne's Center and Reserve contained the army's four artillery companies, four dragoon troops, two company-sized regular infantry units serving as advance and rear guards, four light infantry companies, two of the army's six rifle companies, and the army's three scout companies. Major Henry Burbeck led the four artillery companies. His company commanders were Capt. Mahlon Ford, who had been wounded at Wabash, Capt. Moses Porter, Lt. Percy Pope, another Wabash survivor, and Lt. Ebenezer Massey. Captain Robert Miscampbell, who fell at Fallen Timbers, led the four dragoon troops. Miscampbell led one troop personally, while Capt. Solomon van Rensselaer, who was wounded at the battle, Lt. Leonard Covington, and Lt. John Webb commanded the others.

Individual company commanders led Wayne's regular infantry, light infantry, and rifle companies. Captain John Cooke commanded the Advanced Infantry Guard and Capt. John Reed, who had been wounded at Wabash, the Rear Infantry Guard. Captain Joseph Brock, another Wabash survivor, Capt. Howell Lewis, Capt. Daniel Bradley, and Lt. Bernard Gaines led the four light infantry companies. Captain William Preston and Capt. Daniel Tilton led the two rifle companies.

Captain William Wells, who had led a Miami unit at Wabash, commanded one of the three scout companies. The son-in-law of Little Turtle, he was, William Henry Harrison said, "indispensable to our operation." Wells and his chief subordinate, Lt. Robert McClellan, who would become a celebrated

While serving as Governor of Kentucky, Charles Scott lived in this 1798 Governor's Mansion. A fall in 1808 on its ice-covered front steps left him crippled for the remainder of his life. His last act in office in 1812 was to appoint William Henry Harrison commander of the Kentucky militia to prevent Wilkinson from obtaining the position. (Courtesy of the Kentucky Division of Historic Properties)

explorer of the Pacific Northwest, both were wounded in a skirmish a few days before the battle. The frontiersmen Capt. William Kibbey and Capt. George Shrim commanded the other two scout companies.

Wilkinson led the Right Wing, which consisted of the 1st and 3rd Sublegion units not detached to Wayne's "Center and Reserve." His staff included his aides, Lt. Bartholomew Schaumbaugh, another Wabash survivor, and Lt. Campbell Smith, who would be wounded at Fallen Timbers.

Wilkinson's principal subordinates were Capt. William Peters and Capt. Jacob Kingsbury. Peters led the 1st Sublegion, which consisted of two regular infantry battalions. Capt. Daniel Britt, wounded at Wabash, and Capt. Hamilton Armstrong commanded the battalions. Kingsbury led the 3rd Sublegion, which consisted of two regular infantry battalions and a rifle battalion. Captain William Lewis and Capt. John Heth led the regular infantry battalions. Captain Uriah Springer commanded the rifle battalion and led one of its two companies. Captain Richard Sparks, an adopted Shawnee, led the other.

Hamtramck commanded the Left Wing, which consisted of the 2nd and 4th Sublegion units not detached to the "Center and Reserve." His principal subordinates were Lt. Col. David Strong and Maj. Jonathan Haskell. Strong led the 2nd Sublegion, which consisted of two regular infantry battalions. Captain Edward Miller led one battalion, which included the company of Capt. Richard Greaton, who had been wounded at Wabash. Captain Samuel Andrews led the other battalion.

In the absence of Lt. Col. Thomas Butler, the commandant of Fort Fayette whose wounds at Wabash had left him unable to assume a field command, Haskell led the 4th Sublegion. Lieutenant William Clark, who served as his quartermaster, was a younger brother of George Rogers Clark. In 1804, he and his friend Lt. Meriwether Lewis, who would join Wayne's army after Fallen Timbers, would lead the famous Lewis and Clark expedition to the Pacific Ocean.

The 4th Sublegion consisted of two regular infantry battalions and a rifle battalion. Captain Jacob Slough led one regular infantry battalion. Wounded at Wabash, he would be wounded at Fallen Timbers as well. Captain Maxwell Bines, who also had been wounded at Wabash, led one of the battalion's companies. In the absence of Capt. John Cooke, detached to lead the Advance Infantry Guard, Capt. Benjamin Price, also wounded at Wabash, led the other regular infantry battalion. Captain Alexander Gibson, who led the Americans' successful defense of Fort Recovery before Fallen Timbers, commanded the rifle battalion and led one of its two companies. Captain Edward Butler, who had survived Wabash, led the other. Butler was a brother of Maj. Gen. Richard Butler, who had died at Wabash, and Lt. Col. Thomas Butler.

Major-General Charles Scott led the Kentucky horsemen with Wayne's army. Scott's principal subordinates commanded his two brigades. Brigadier-General Robert Todd led the Northern Kentucky Brigade. His principal subordinates, who commanded his three battalions, were Maj. William Price, Maj. Notley Conn, and Maj. William Russell. Brigadier-General Thomas Barbee led the Southern Kentucky Brigade. His three battalion commanders were Maj. Aquila Whittaker, Maj. John Caldwell, and Maj. Nathan Houston. The celebrated frontiersman Capt. Brand Ballard led one of Whittaker's companies.

INDIAN AND CANADIAN

The Indian army had no command structure similar to that of the Americans. A council of the most prominent Indian war leaders first agreed on general strategy and tactics. They then led specific units during battle.

At the extreme left end of the Indian line, **Egushwa**, who had succeeded the famous Pontiac as Ottawa war leader, and **Little Otter** (Nekeik), the victorious commander at Lowry's Run, led the Ottawa. Both would be wounded at the battle. With them fought small numbers of Potawatomi, led by Le Petit Bled, and Ojibwe, under an unknown commander.

The Shawnee, Delaware, and Miami fought in the center of the Indian line. **Blue Jacket** (Waweyapiersenwaw), the leading Shawnee commander, sometimes is said to have commanded the Indian army. Other important Shawnee leaders at the battle included Black Hoof (Catecahassa), who had led the Shawnee at Peckuwe, Black Fish (Cottawamago), and the young Shawnee commander Tecumseh. Buckongahelas, Capt. Pipe (Hopocan), and Big Cat (Whangypushies) led the Delaware. Little Turtle (Mishikinakwa), architect of the Indian victory at Wabash, led the Miami.

This colored lithograph from Mckenney and Hall's 1855 *The Indian Tribes of North America* reproduces a now-lost Charles Bird King portrait of the Shawnee chief Black Hoof. (Author's collection)

The Wyandots fought at the right of the Indian line. **Tarhe**, who led the Wyandots, would be wounded at the battle. The younger commander Roundhead (Stiahta) later would become the leading Wyandot war leader. Small numbers of Mingos and Mohawks fought with the Wyandots under unknown commanders.

At the extreme right of the Indian line, **Capt. William Caldwell** led two companies of Canadian volunteers dressed as Indians. During the Revolutionary War, his company of Butler's Rangers, a loyalist unit, had fought with the Ohio Indians from 1778 through 1782. Captain Daniel McKillip, who led one of Caldwell's companies, fell at the battle. Captain Charles Smith, clerk of the Western District, Upper Canada, Court of Common Pleas, led the other company.

Captain William Caldwell's sword, scabbard, and belt are displayed at Fort Malden National Historic Site in Amherstburg, Ontario. (Parks Canada Agency)

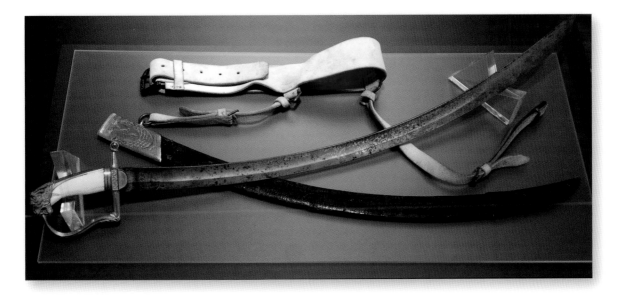

OPPOSING ARMIES

AMERICAN

The American army that fought at Fallen Timbers, which Wayne called "the Federal Army," contained about 1,800 US Army and 1,500 Kentucky volunteer officers and soldiers. The units from the US Army were artillery, dragoon, regular infantry, light infantry, rifle, and scout formations. The Kentucky units all contained irregular horsemen.

In 1792, Secretary of War Henry Knox reorganized the US army as the Legion of the United States, a force of 4,500 officers and men, divided into four sublegions capable of fighting independently. Each sublegion, led by a brigadier-general, was to contain an artillery company and dragoon troop, each led by a captain. It also was to have two regular infantry battalions and one rifle battalion, each led by a major. Each battalion was to contain four companies led by captains.

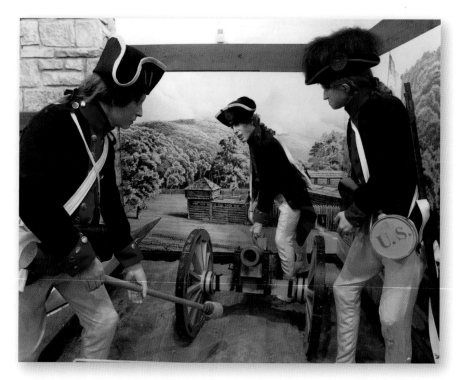

These figures at the Fort Recovery State Museum in Fort Recovery, Ohio, are operating a reproduction of one of what Wilkinson called the army's "popgun howitzers." (Courtesy of the Ohio Historical Society. Photograph by David R. Barker)

At the time of the battle, Knox's organizational structure still existed on paper. The Legion, however, had less than half its assigned numbers. It also had only a fraction of its assigned units, often led by junior officers. At Fallen Timbers, the sublegions had little operational significance. By the time of the battle, Wayne had organized the Legion's artillery, dragoon, regular infantry, light infantry, rifle, and scout units into three large formations. The first was a 900-man "Center and Reserve," led personally by Wayne. The second was a 450-man "Right Wing," which contained the 1st and 3rd Sublegion regular infantry and rifle units not detached to the Center and Reserve. The third was a 450-man "Left Wing," which contained the 2nd and 4th Sublegion regular infantry and rifle units not in the Center and Reserve.

These artillery shells, recovered from the site of Fort Greeneville, are displayed at the Garst Museum in Greenville, Ohio. (Author's photograph)

The 120 Legion artillerymen were in Wayne's Center and Reserve. Organized into four companies, they had 16 guns. St. Clair's army had been hindered by the need to transport artillery carriages on wagon roads. Wayne wanted guns that could be carried on horseback. His 2.75- and 2.85-caliber King howitzers, especially manufactured for the Legion, had 50lb brass barrels and 150–75lb. carriages that could be carried by packhorses in special saddles.

Wayne's howitzers could function as either field guns or mortars. Operated by a team consisting of an officer, two gunners, and six soldiers, each could fire as often as every 15 seconds an iron or stone ball, or a hollow shell filled with explosives that detonated at a distance determined by the length of the shell's fuse.

Against infantry at close range, the howitzers usually fired canvas bags or tin canisters filled with iron or lead balls of about .30 to .35 caliber. After the bag or canister dissolved on firing, about 30 balls went forward in a geometrically expanding disk. Canvas bags, usually called "grapeshot," were used against infantry at distances of about 400yds. Tin canisters were used at closer ranges.

The Legion's about 200 dragoons were also in the Center and Reserve. They were organized into four units called the Bay, Black, Gray, and Sorrell Horse Troops. Each troop had four squads of about 15 men. The dragoons carried sabers and 1763 Charleville carbines, short-barreled muskets that could be fired on horseback, and used bugles for communication.

The Legion had about 830 regular infantrymen. About 150, detached to the Advance and Rear Regular Infantry Guards, were in the Center and Reserve. The other 680, which Wayne called the "Battalion Infantry," remained in the Wings. There each sublegion had two battalions, each with either two or three small companies. The 1st and 3rd Sublegions each had only about 120 infantrymen, and the 2nd and 4th about 220.

The regular infantrymen carried 1766 and 1774 Charleville muskets, 69-caliber weapons that could kill with lead balls men hundreds of yards away. Most men could learn to use their muskets to hit targets the size of a man at about 50yds. The weapons, however, were designed to be fired in mass barrages, in which trained men could fire their weapons as fast as every 20 seconds.

To prepare his flintlock musket for firing, an infantryman uncovered the firing pan, bit a cartridge, poured powder from the cartridge into the pan, and closed the pan. He then rammed into the barrel the cartridge, which contained the remaining powder and the projectiles to be fired. When he pulled the trigger, the flint struck the frizzen and uncovered the firing pan. Sparks from the striking flint ignited the powder in the pan. Fire from the resulting explosion moved through the touch hole. When it ignited the powder in the barrel, that explosion expelled the projectiles. (Author's drawing)

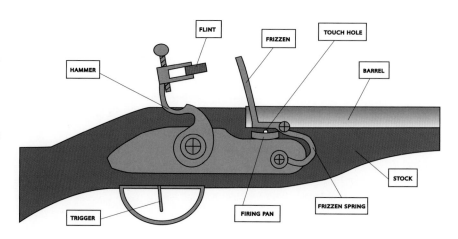

American regular infantrymen usually carried 24 cartridges, wrapped paper tubes containing a ball and the powder for one firing. Wayne, who thought that his muskets would be more effective in the woods if they fired more projectiles, ordered the cartridges altered "to contain one ball and three buck shot at least." The shot was of about .30 caliber.

Each infantryman also had a bayonet, which could be attached to his musket's barrel by a metal ring. When fitted with bayonets, the muskets could be fired, but not quickly reloaded. Although massed musket fire had little effect on Indians in the western woods, tomahawks could not resist bayonets.

The Legion's 200 light infantrymen, organized into four companies, were also in Wayne's Center and Reserve. The light infantrymen, whom he called his "improved musketeers," carried special weapons for fighting the Indians and, like the dragoons, bugles for transmitting orders for movements through the woods. Their special weapons were modified muskets and cartridges. Experiments by the innovative American commander revealed that, if the touchhole in a Charleville musket was enlarged and bored at a different angle, and the powder placed in its barrel was sufficiently fine, the sparks created when its flint struck its frizzen could ignite the powder in the barrel. Soldiers armed with Wayne's modified muskets were issued special cartridges with fine powder. The cartridges, moreover, were altered to contain "a heavy buckshot without ball."

Wayne's "improved musketeers" could load and fire their weapons rapidly, without using their muskets' firing pans. Armed with, in effect, shotguns with attached bayonets, they would perform a dual role at Fallen Timbers. They first would delay advancing Indians by firing loads of at least nine shot of about .30 caliber. Then, when the American battle line went forward, they would join the regular infantrymen in advancing with bayonets.

The Legion also had about 360 riflemen organized into six companies. Two rifle companies, along with the light infantry companies, formed the army's Advance and Rear Irregular Guards, which were in the Center and Reserve. The other four served in the Wings, where the 3rd and 4th Sublegions each had a two-company rifle battalion.

American riflemen carried firearms of about .52 caliber. Those who were minimally competent could hit targets the size of a man's head at 100yds. Their weapons, however, took twice as long to load as muskets, could not use cartridges, and did not have bayonets. Wayne, who believed that rifles were "only useful in the hands of real riflemen," assigned to his rifle companies riflemen who could hit a man at 200yds. He remedied their lack of bayonets by issuing bayonet-tipped wooden sticks, which could be unfolded and locked to form spears. Some of the riflemen also carried bugles for transmitting orders.

Wayne also retained under his personal command about 90 scouts. Usually called "spies," they were organized into three companies. Wayne's superb scout companies included men who had lived as Indians, like William Wells, and unusually skilled frontiersmen like Robert McClellan. They carried rifles or muskets, and also tomahawks and knives.

At Wabash, the Indians had targeted the American officers, and then killed masses of leaderless soldiers. Wayne issued an order before Fallen Timbers designed to reduce officer casualties. The first modified their dress: "It is to be decidedly and clearly understood by the officers," he announced, "that they are to dress as nearly as may be, in the same uniform, hats and caps with the soldiers belonging to their respective corps."

Wayne also changed the weapons that officers were to carry. Those with ranks of at least major, who commanded on horseback, would retain their usual swords and pistols. His commanding captains and more junior officers, however, were to carry the same weapons as non-commissioned officers: espontoons, pointed blades atop staffs 6ft 2in. long.

The high quality of Wayne's officers and the long period available for training, allowed him to give his soldiers elaborate preparation for combat. The Americans who fought at Fallen Timbers had learned to use their weapons effectively. Their experience included mock battles with men dressed as Indians, who fought using Indian tactics and weapons.

About 1,500 Kentucky volunteer horsemen also fought in the Federal Army. After Wabash, Congress had enacted the Militia Act of 1792, which required the states to organize and equip their militia forces so that they could act as supplemental US Army forces in infantry regiments, artillery companies, and dragoon troops. By the time of Fallen Timbers, Kentucky had organized its militia into such units.

Wayne, however, did not want such men. He asked instead for mounted volunteers. Kentuckians experienced in Indian warfare, veterans of many expeditions on horseback into the Ohio woods, preferred to fight as horsemen. Such men, Wayne wrote to Knox, could serve as valuable "auxiliaries to the regular dragoons."

On May 17, 1794, Knox authorized Maj. Gen. Charles Scott of the Kentucky militia to recruit 2,000 volunteer horsemen who would be paid by the United States. Those at Fallen Timbers were in two units, recruited north and south of the Kentucky River. Brigadier-General Robert Todd's Northern Kentucky Brigade had about 700 men in its three four-company battalions. Brigadier-General Thomas Barbee's Southern Kentucky Brigade had about 800 men in its three four-company battalions. Before Fallen Timbers, Todd's Brigade was reorganized to create a 150-man battalion led by Maj. William Price, which served as the army's forwardmost advance guard.

Although mounted, the Kentuckians were otherwise very different from Wayne's saber-wielding dragoons. Dressed in frontier clothing rather than uniforms, they fought as riflemen. For close combat, they carried tomahawks, and butcher's or other knives.

INDIAN AND CANADIAN

About 1,100 Indians and Canadians fought at Fallen Timbers. The 1,000 Indians, who fought as volunteers, were generally organized by tribes. The tribes were subdivided into smaller units of about 60. Each contained three units of about 20 men. They commenced the battle in a slightly curving line, in which they were dispersed six deep.

The tribes spoke languages of two types, Iroquoian and Algonquian. The tribes that spoke Iroquoian languages fought together at the right of the Indian line. They were Wyandots, Mingos, and a few Mohawks.

The Wyandots were a product of the Beaver Wars, which destroyed or displaced several groups in southern Ontario that called themselves the Wendat. Those who fled northeast became known as the Huron. Those who fled west and ultimately settled in Ohio, were called the Wyandot. The Mingo also were a product of the Beaver Wars, when the tribes of the Iroquois confederacy had attempted to incorporate thousands of defeated enemies. Many descendants of imperfectly assimilated captives, and of Catholic Mohawks who had separated from their tribe, ultimately moved to Ohio, where they became known as the Mingo. By 1792, the Mingo were losing their separate identity and soon would be known as Seneca, one of the tribes of the Iroquois confederacy. A small number of Mohawks also fought at Fallen Timbers. They were from the Grand River, in Upper Canada, to which they had fled after the Revolutionary War. A much larger party, led by Joseph Brant, reached the Maumee too late to fight in the battle. 97

The Algonquian-language speakers included the Shawnee, Delaware, and Miami, who formed the center of the Indian line, and the Anishinabe, a confederacy of the Ojibwe, Ottawa, and Potawatomi who fought on the Indian left. The Ojibwe, often called Chippewa, had five subgroups. Those who fought at the battle probably were from the Missisauga subgroup, which was often considered a separate tribe. The Potawatomi were from villages near the mouth of the St. Joseph River on Lake Michigan.

The Miami warriors at Fallen Timbers probably included Little Turtle's nephew, Jean Baptiste de Richardville (Piniwa). Richardville, who later became principal chief of the Miami, died in 1841 at his house in Fort Wayne, which is now a museum. (Photograph courtesy of Allen County-Fort Wayne Historical Society)

The Indians usually were merciless enemies, who fought the Americans just as they fought one another. They preserved to varying degrees ancient customs on the treatment of captives, who became the property of the warriors who took them. Prisoners usually were adopted or enslaved. Adult males, however, and also females, sometimes were tortured to death and even ritually eaten.

The Indians sought to intimidate potential enemies by demonstrating the spectacular savagery that foes might expect. Their reputation for cruelty, and their terrifying appearance when painted for battle, gave them a psychological advantage over Americans who had not fought them before. Even those who were not intimidated had the highest respect for their skill in battle. They were, William Henry Harrison judged, "the finest light infantry troops in the world."

The Indians were elaborately trained in the skills needed for warfare in the Ohio woods. From boyhood, they learned to ignore extremes of temperature, to endure hunger and thirst, and to survive alone for indefinite periods. At 12, they began training in combat skills and small unit maneuvers. At 14, they began participating in raids. Most who fought at Fallen Timbers were veterans of many engagements.

Their spectacular success at Wabash had left the Indians supremely confident. They attributed their many victories over the British and Americans to the superior quality of their warriors. Many believed that they could defeat any number of Americans, armed with any weapons, on any field.

The Indians carried a variety of firearms. Those included smoothbore and rifled weapons of different calibers, including muskets, rifles, and fusils, small muskets usually used for hunting. They typically used their firearms to fire multiple projectiles, often rounds of one large ball and three smaller balls of as little as .25 caliber. Many carried the standard weapon used by British infantry, the Land Pattern Musket. That .75-caliber weapon, often called a "Brown Bess" musket, was generally similar in range, accuracy, and reliability to the Charleville muskets of the Americans. For close combat, most Indians used tomahawks. Some carried wooden clubs, often elaborately carved and decorated, and sometimes studded with iron blades. All also carried knives.

About 70 Canadians from the Detroit area fought with the Indians. Because Britain was not at war with the United States, the Canadians, who were either experienced frontiersmen or loyalist fugitives who had emigrated west, volunteered to fight covertly. Dressed as Indians, they were organized into Capt. William Caldwell's two "Volunteer Companies of Refugees." Many had fought in Ohio during the Revolutionary War in Caldwell's company of Col. John Butler's regiment of loyalist rangers. They carried the weapons of Canadian militiamen, British Land Pattern muskets with bayonets.

This Ottawa war club, from the period of Fallen Timbers, may have been used at the battle. (Courtesy of Allen County-Fort Wayne Historical Society)

ORDERS OF BATTLE

AMERICAN (3,300)[1]

Maj. Gen. Anthony Wayne, Commander
Capt. Thomas Lewis, Aide de camp
Capt. Henry De Butts, Aide de camp
Lt. William Henry Harrison, Aide de camp
James O'Hara, Quartermaster General
Maj. John Mills, Adjutant General

Center and detached (900)	Maj. Gen. Anthony Wayne
Advance Infantry Guard (3rd and 4th Sublegions) (75)	Capt. John Cooke
Rear Infantry Guard (1st and 2nd Sublegions) (75)	Capt. John Reed
Advance Irregular Guard (120)	Capt. Howell Lewis
Light Infantry Company of Capt. Howell Lewis (50)	
Rifle Company of Capt. Thomas Lewis (D) (70)	Capt. Daniel Tilton, Acting Commander
Rear Irregular Guard (120) Capt. Daniel Bradley	
Light Infantry Company of Capt. Daniel Bradley (50)	
Rifle Company of Capt. William Preston (70)	
Dragoon Squadron (200)	Capt. Robert Miscampbell (K)
Bay Horse Troop (50)	Lt. Leonard Covington, Acting Commander
Black Horse Troop (50)	Capt. Robert Miscampbell (K)
Gray Horse Troop (50)	Lt. John Webb
Sorrell Horse Troop (50)	Capt. Solomon Van Rensselaer (W)
US Artillery Companies (120) (16 3lb howitzers)	Maj. Henry Burbeck
Company of Capt. Mahlon Ford	
Company of Lt. Percy Pope	
Company of Capt. Moses Porter	
Company of Lt. Ebenezer Massey	
Light Infantry Company of Capt. Jacob Kingsbury (D) (50)	Lt. Bernard Gaines, Acting Commander
Light Infantry Company of Capt. Joseph Brock (50)	
Scout Company of Capt. William Kibbey (65)	
Scout Company of Capt. George Shrim (15)	
Scout Company of Capt. William Wells (10)	

Left Wing (450)	Lt. Col. John Hamtramck
2nd Sublegion (120)	Lt. Col. David Strong
1st Infantry Battalion (60) (2 Cos.)	Capt. Edward Miller
2nd Infantry Battalion (60) (2 Cos.)	Capt. Samuel Andrews
4th Sublegion (330)	Maj. Jonathan Haskell, Acting Commander
1st Infantry Battalion (110) (3 Cos.)	Capt. Jacob Slough (W)
2nd Infantry Battalion (110) (3 Cos.)	Capt. John Cooke (D), Capt. Benjamin Price, Acting Commander
Rifle Battalion (110)	Capt. Alexander Gibson
Company Of Capt. Alexander Gibson (55)	
Company Of Capt. Edward Butler (55)	

Right Wing (450)	Brig. Gen. James Wilkinson
1st Sublegion (120)	Lt. Col. John Hamtramck (D) Capt. William Peters, Acting Commander
1st Infantry Battalion (60) (2 Cos.)	Capt. Hamilton Armstrong
2nd Infantry Battalion (60) (2 Cos.)	Capt. Daniel Britt

3rd Sublegion (330)	Capt. Jacob Kingsbury, Acting Commander
1st Infantry Battalion (110) (3 Cos.)	Capt. John Heth
2nd Infantry Battalion (110) (3 Cos.)	Capt. William Lewis
Rifle Battalion (110)	Capt. Uriah Springer
Company Of Capt. Uriah Springer (55)	
Company Of Capt. Richard Sparks (55)	
Kentucky Mounted Volunteers (1,500)	**Maj. Gen. Charles Scott**
Northern Kentucky Brigade (700)	Brig. Gen. Robert Todd
Advance Scout Battalion (150) (2 Cos.)	Maj. William Price
Battalion Of Maj. Notley Conn (275) (4 Cos.)	
Battalion Of Maj. William Russell (275) (4 Cos.)	
Southern Kentucky Brigade (800)	Brig. Gen. Thomas Barbee
Battalion Of Maj. Aquila Whitaker (270) (4 Cos.)	
Battalion Of Maj John Caldwell (270) (4 Cos.)	
Battalion Of Maj. Nathan Houston (260) (4 Cos.)	

INDIAN AND CANADIAN (1,100)[2]

Left Wing (275)	
Ojibwe (25)	Unknown Commander
Ottawa (225)	Egushwa (W) and Little Otter (W)
Potawatomi (25)	Le Pett Bled
Center (500)	
Shawnee (200)	Blue Jacket, Black Hoof, and Black Fish
Delaware (200)	Buckongahelas, Capt. Pipe, and Big Cat
Miami (80)	Little Turtle
Right Wing (345)	
Mingo and Mohawks (25)	Unknown Commander
Wyandot (250)	Tarhe (W)
Volunteer Companies Of Refugees (70)	Capt. William Caldwell
Company Of Capt. Daniel Mckillip (K) (50)	
Company Of Capt. Charles Smith (20)	

Notes

1. The surviving records provide incomplete and conflicting information on American numbers, units and commanders at Fallen Timbers. In this reconstruction, the numbers in the American army and in individual units are estimates. Some identified battalion and acting commanders may be inaccurate.
2. Contemporary estimates of the number of Indians present in the Indian line at the commencement of the battle ranged from 900 to 1,200. Additional Indians reached the field during the battle. Numbers in individual units are estimates based upon conflicting contemporary sources.

Killed or mortally wounded (K)
Wounded (W)
Not Present (NP)
Detached for other service (D)

OPPOSING PLANS

AMERICAN PLANS

The initial object of Wayne's campaign was to build and garrison a permanent fort at Kekionga, an abandoned complex of Indian villages at the head of the Maumee River. The site, at what is now Fort Wayne, Indiana, controlled the most important travel route in the Northwest Territory. From it, the Maumee flowed to Lake Erie, and 8-mile long Hamilton's Road led to the Little Wabash River, which flowed to the Wabash and the Ohio.

St. Clair's army had advanced 97 miles from Fort Washington toward Kekionga. Its experience had revealed the logistical difficulties Wayne's army would face in operating in the Ohio wilderness. American soldiers consumed daily rations of beef and bread. Herds of oxen moving with an army could provide the beef, which would be slaughtered at a daily rate of about a head for every 100 men. The flour for bread could be provided either by wagons or packhorses.

Wagons, however, could move in the Ohio wilderness only on wagon roads. Construction of such roads required the laborious leveling of trees to foot-high stumps, and construction of bridges over streams and gullies. On rough roads in the wilderness, wagons could move at only 1–2 miles per hour, and their fragile axles and wheels often collapsed.

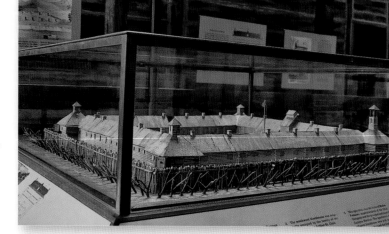

Rufus Putnam, whose fort overlooking Boston had forced the British to evacuate the city in 1776, designed for the Marietta settlers Campus Martius, a fortress impregnable to Indian attack. This model is at the Campus Martius Museum of the Northwest Territory, where Putnam's 1788 house, a part of the fort, survives on its original site in Marietta, Ohio. (Photograph by Wendy S. Winkler)

The lower Ohio River frontier in 1792

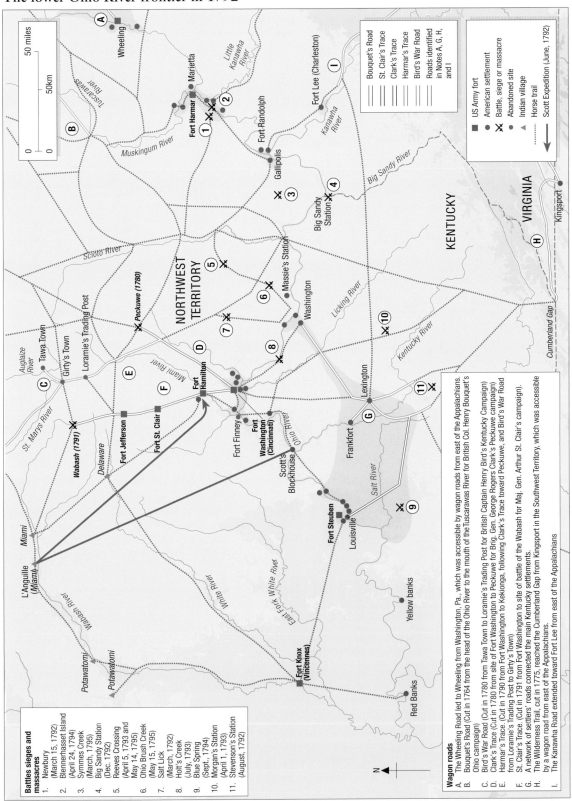

Legend:

Roads:
- Bouquet's Road
- St. Clair's Trace
- Clark's Trace
- Harmar's Trace
- Bird's War Road
- Roads identified in Notes A, G, H, and I

Symbols:
- ■ US Army fort
- ● American settlement
- ✗ Battle, siege or massacre
- ○ Abandoned site
- ▲ Indian village
- ···· Horse trail
- → Scott Expedition (June, 1792)

Battles sieges and massacres
1. Newbury (March 15, 1792)
2. Blennerhasset Island (April 24, 1794)
3. Symmes Creek (March, 1795)
4. Big Sandy Station (Dec. 1792)
5. Reeves Crossing (April 5, 1793 and May 14, 1795)
6. Ohio Brush Creek (May 15, 1795)
7. Salt Lick
8. Holt's Creek (March, 1792)
9. Blue Spring (July, 1793)
10. Morgan's Station (Sept., 1794)
11. Stevenson's Station (April 1, 1793)

Wagon roads

A. The Wheeling Road led to Wheeling from Washington, Pa., which was accessible by wagon roads from east of the Appalachians.

B. Bouquet's Road (Cut in 1764 from the head of the Ohio River to the mouth of the Tuscarawas River for British Col. Henry Bouquet's Ohio campaign)

C. Bird's War Road (Cut in 1780 from Tawa Town to Loramie's Trading Post for British Captain Henry Bird's Kentucky Campaign)

D. Clark's Trace (Cut in 1780 from site of Fort Washington to Peckuwe for Brig. Gen. George Rogers Clark's Peckuwe campaign)

E. Harmar's Trace. (Cut in 1790 from Fort Washington to Kekionga, following Clark's Trace toward Peckuwe, and Bird's War Road from Loramie's Trading Post to Girty's Town)

F. St. Clair's Trace. (Cut in 1791 from Fort Washington to site of battle of the Wabash for Maj. Gen. Arthur St. Clair's campaign).

G. A network of settlers' roads connected the main Kentucky settlements.

H. The Wilderness Trail, cut in 1775, reached the Cumberland Gap from Kingsport in the Southwest Territory, which was accessible by a wagon road from east of the Appalachians.

I. The Kanawha Road extended toward Fort Lee from east of the Appalachians.

Map labels: Wheeling, Little Kanawha River, Tuscarawas River, Fort Lee (Charleston), Fort Harmar, Marietta, Muskingum River, Fort Randolph, Kanawha River, Gallipolis, Big Sandy River, Scioto River, Big Sandy Station, NORTHWEST TERRITORY, Peckuwe (1780), Massie's Station, KENTUCKY, Licking River, Washington, Tawa Town, Girty's Town, Loramie's Trading Post, Auglaize River, Kentucky River, St. Marys River, Miami River, Fort Hamilton, Lexington, VIRGINIA, Kingsport, Cumberland Gap, Wabash (1791), Fort Jefferson, Fort St. Clair, Fort Finney, Fort Washington (Cincinnati), Ohio River, Scott's Blockhouse, Frankfort, Salt River, Delaware, L'Anguille (Miami), Miami, Potawatomi, Potawatomi, Wabash River, White River, East Fork White River, Fort Steuben, Louisville, Yellow banks, Fort Knox (Vincennes), Red Banks

Scale: 50 miles / 50km

N

Wayne's new geographical information appeared for the first time in Bradley and Harrison's 1796 *A Map of the United States*. This detail from the map shows his area of operations. (Library of Congress, Geography and Map Division)

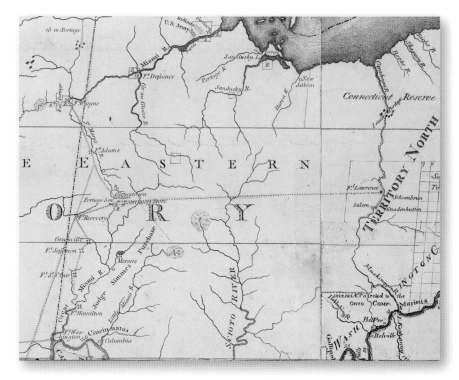

Packhorses using special saddles each could carry four 50lb kegs of flour about 25 miles a day. That, however, was the daily flour ration for only about 100 men. The available horses, which lacked stamina, had to be replaced after carrying supplies a few hundred miles.

Oxen and horses also required food. Able to carry only about a six-day supply for themselves, they could not move far unless they could find adequate forage along their route. They could transport supplies only on routes with such forage and only in seasons when it was available.

St. Clair's army had almost starved before being massacred. It was doubtful, moreover, that it could have been fed even if it had reached Kekionga. "It is next to impossible," Wayne wrote to Knox on March 3, 1794, " to supply a large body of troops so far advanced in an uncultivated and savage wilderness for any length of time by means of pack horses or land carriage only."

In 1792, Brig. Gen. Rufus Putnam proposed a plan for Wayne's campaign that would make it easier to provide food supplies to the American army. The Americans, he argued, should follow Bouquet's Road from Fort Fayette to abandoned Fort Laurens. The Tuscarawas River, a short portage, and the Cuyahoga River then led to Lake Erie, from which the Maumee could be ascended to Kekionga. By that route Wayne's army and the garrison at Kekionga could be supplied largely by water.

Knox rejected Putnam's plan. American activity on Lake Erie, he concluded, might provoke a war with Britain. From his study of Putnam's plan, however, Wayne ultimately reached an important conclusion. He could advance to Kekionga, and later supply a fort there, by different routes.

By 1794, Wayne would have a basis for preparing a final plan unavailable to his ill-fated predecessor. His superb corps of scouts had provided accurate geographical information about his area of operations. Wayne concluded

The photograph shows reproductions of a keelboat (left) and pirogue (right) used by Wayne's lieutenants Meriwether Lewis and William Clark during their 1804 expedition to the Pacific Ocean. (Courtesy of US Army Center of Military History)

from that information that he should build two permanent forts on the Maumee. One, to be called Fort Defiance, would be at the mouth of the Auglaize River. The other, Fort Wayne, would be at Kekionga.

When water was high in the spring and fall, Forts Defiance and Wayne could be supplied largely by water. Keelboats, powered by sails or oars at about 3mph, could carry supplies from Fort Hamilton up the Miami River and Loramie Creek to the site of Loramie's Trading Post. From there, Hartshorne's Road led to Girty's Town on the St. Marys River and Bird's War Road on to Tawa Town on the Auglaize. Flatboats and pirogues, large canoes that could carry 2,000lb loads, could transport supplies down the St. Marys, Auglaize, and Maumee Rivers, and keelboats up the Maumee.

After his campaign, Wayne concluded, he would use that network of alternative water routes to supply his forts on the Maumee. He would build a new series of forts to protect the routes. He then could abandon the existing Forts St. Clair, Jefferson, Greeneville, and Recovery, which could be supplied only by land.

The American commander nonetheless decided to advance to Kekionga by land. If the logistical difficulties could be overcome for a sufficient period, a land campaign would increase the chances that his army would fight a decisive battle with the Ohio Indians. An American victory in such a battle, Wayne believed, would end the war on the Ohio River frontier.

By 1794, Wayne had advanced his army to Fort Greeneville. His new geographical information allowed him to choose a deceptive route from there to the Maumee that would diminish the ability of the Indians to assemble a large force to oppose him. After first marching toward Kekionga, he would advance quickly to the Glaize. After building a fort there, he would march up the Maumee to Kekionga, build a fort there, and return to Fort Greeneville.

This portion of Wayne's trace between the army's fourth and fifth camps, survives as a county road near Camden, Ohio. (Author's photograph)

The construction of British Fort Miamis on the Maumee in 1794 complicated Wayne's plan. It also extended the period his campaign would require. After building a fort at the Glaize, Wayne decided that his army would have to go down the Maumee to the British fort and, if necessary, reduce it before going up the Maumee to Kekionga.

For such an extended campaign, his army would require a three–four month supply of food. By careful planning, Wayne and Quartermaster General James O'Hara were barely able to provide food for the necessary period by wagons and packhorses. Their logistical study revealed that wagons should not carry more than 1,600lb loads, that packhorse convoys could advance more quickly if not accompanied by wagons, and that if convoys were too small their guards would consume the convoys' food before they reached their destination.

The Indians, Wayne knew, might attack while his army was encamped. The Americans would build 33 camps, and use three twice. Crude breastworks of logs piled about 4ft high would surround the 600yds-square camps. The areas around them would be cleared for 200yds to open lines of fire.

The upper Ohio River frontier and Upper Canada in 1792

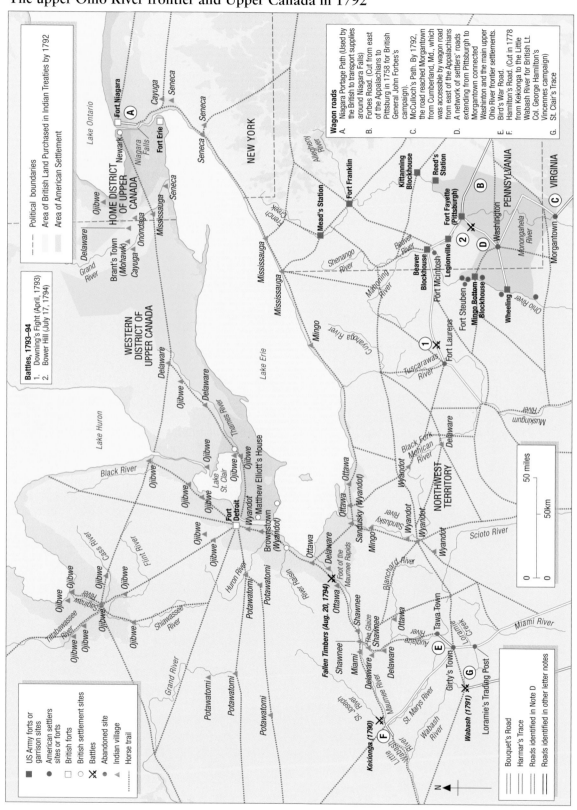

Political boundaries
- Area of British Land Purchased in Indian Treaties by 1792
- Area of American Settlement

Battles, 1793–94
1. Downing's Fight (April, 1793)
2. Bower Hill (July 17, 1794)

Wagon roads

A. Niagara Portage Path (Used by the British to transport supplies around Niagara Falls)
B. Forbes Road. (Cut from east of the Appalachians to Pittsburg in 1758 for British General John Forbes's campaign).
   McCulloch's Path. By 1792, the road reached Morgantown from Cumberland, Md., which was accessible by wagon road from east of the Appalachians.
D. A network of settlers' roads extending from Pittsburgh to Morgantown connected Washington and the main upper Ohio River frontier settlements.
E. Bird's War Road.
F. Hamilton's Road. (Cut in 1778 from Kekionga to the Little Wabash River for British Lt. Col. George Hamilton's Vincennes campaign)
G. St. Clair's Trace

Legend:
- ■ US Army forts or garrison sites
- ● American settlers sites or forts
- □ British forts
- ○ British settlement sites
- ✕ Battles
- ○ Abandoned site
- ▲ Indian village
- ·········· Horse trail

Bouquet's Road
Harmar's Trace
Roads identified in Note D
Roads identified in other letter notes

50 miles
50km

N

Labels on map:

Lake Ontario
Fort Niagara
Newark
Fort Erie
Niagara Falls
Cayuga
Seneca
Seneca
Seneca
Seneca
Seneca
Ojibwe
HOME DISTRICT OF UPPER CANADA
Mississauga
Onondaga
Cayuga
Mohawk — Brant's Town
Delaware
Grand River
NEW YORK
Allegheny River
French Creek
Fort Franklin
Mead's Station
Kittanning Blockhouse
Reed's Station
Fort Fayette (Pittsburgh)
PENNSYLVANIA
Washington
VIRGINIA
Morgantown
Monongahela River
Beaver River
Beaver Blockhouse
Legionville
Fort McIntosh
Shenango River
Mississauga
Mahoning River
Fort Steuben
Mingo Bottom Blockhouse
Wheeling
Ohio River
WESTERN DISTRICT OF UPPER CANADA
Delaware
Delaware
Cuyahoga River
Mingo
Fort Laurens
Tuscarawas River
Lake Erie
Thames River
Ojibwe
Lake Huron
Black River
Lake St. Clair
Fort Detroit
Matthew Elliott's House
Browstown (Wyandot)
Wyandot
Muskingum River
NORTHWEST TERRITORY
Black Fork Mohican River
Wyandot
Wyandot
Wyandot
Delaware
Sandusky River
Sandusky (Wyandot)
Ottawa
Ottawa
Ottawa
Ottawa
Scioto River
Cass River
Flint River
Huron River
River Raisin
Foot of the Maumee Rapids
Fallen Timbers (Aug. 20, 1794)
Shawnee
The Glaize
Shawnee
Shawnee
Miami
Maumee River
Delaware
Delaware
Auglaize River
Tawa Town
Loramie Creek
Miami River
Blanchard River
St. Joseph River
St. Marys River
Girty's Town
Loramie's Trading Post
Wabash (1791)
Kekionga (1790)
Little Wabash River
Wabash River
Shiawassee River
Tittabawassee River
Saginaw River
Ojibwe
Potawatomi
Potawatomi
Potawatomi
Potawatomi
Grand River

35

The Indians also might attack while the army was marching. The US Army's operational handbook, Friedrich von Steuben's *Regulations*, specified how commanders were to respond to such an attack. American soldiers were to march in at least two columns more than 100yds apart, proceeding in two files. If attacked, a column was to become a two-rank battle line, or retire to the parallel column, where a stronger battle line could be formed. In such lines, American muskets and artillery could fire thousands of balls a minute, and send hundreds of bayonets forward in charges.

Wabash, however, had proven that Indians tactics could defeat the response that Steuben's *Regulations* prescribed. To counter them, Wayne devised complex plans for march and battle. His army would advance with its units widely dispersed, forming a body too large for the Indians to surround. When the Indians attacked from a specific direction, his light infantry units would form a cushion to absorb the onslaught. That cushion would collapse into a battle line formed by the remainder of the army, which would be too long for the Indians to outflank. When that line was formed, the Americans would counterattack. Dragoons and riflemen would assault the Indian flanks. Regular and light infantrymen then would advance with bayonets from the American center. Horsemen, circling far around the Indian right flank, then would attack the retreating Indians, and turn their defeat into a rout.

INDIAN AND CANADIAN PLANS

Communications and logistical restraints limited the ability of the Indians to conduct offensive operations. They could not assemble armies of more than a few hundred warriors quickly. Such armies, moreover, could not operate for long far from Indian bases of food supply, nor fight long with firearms without British supplies of gunpowder. If, however, even a large American army advanced far enough toward their bases of supply, the Indians could field a force capable of defeating it. At Wabash, what appeared to be an undisciplined horde had destroyed a larger American army. The Indians' movements at the battle, moreover, had seemed to defeat American tactics with effortless ease.

The Indian experience of war had been of unrestrained conflicts between Indian groups. In those conflicts, opposing groups had tried to kill or capture as many enemies as possible, including women and children. Because their groups were small, Indian operational doctrines emphasized above all avoidance of casualties. The Indians therefore tried to avoid engagements in which enemies could oppose them on even terms. Raids and massacres of deceived enemies were preferred. No action that would minimize Indian casualties was rejected as dishonorable or immoral.

When battles were unavoidable, the dense western forests provided fields upon which few usually fell. Experience in such battles had taught the Indians that fighting dispersed could reduce casualties further. They also had learned that the ratio of losses was most favorable when an enemy force was surrounded. Even when heavily outnumbered, the Indians always tried to surround an enemy in a circle of dispersed warriors. If a surrounded enemy attacked a segment of the circle, the Indians there fell back and enlarged the circle. If the attacking force advanced far enough, the Indians tried to surround it in a separate, smaller circle.

Colonel Henry Bouquet, the only British commander to defeat the Indians in a significant engagement, warned of the effectiveness of Indian tactics in a battle in the western woods. A British or American commander, he wrote, "cannot discover them tho from every tree, log or bush, he receives an incessant fire … He will not hesitate to charge those invisible enemies, but he will charge in vain … He will find himself surrounded by a circle of fire, which, like an artificial horizon, follows him everywhere."

At Wabash, the Indians had applied their tactics on an unprecedented scale. Their initial attack had disrupted the formation of the American lines and reduced the numbers that would fight in the lines' units. Their encirclement had left the compressed American soldiers targets rather than sources of devastating firepower. After retreating before American bayonet charges, they had cut off and killed soldiers who had advanced too far. The Indians' circle of fire had burned at Wabash until the US Army had ceased to exist.

The Miami commander Little Turtle, architect of the victory at Wabash, was aware that Indian tactics were difficult to apply in large engagements. Despite planning by experienced commanders and execution by disciplined warriors, the movements needed to execute them over a large area could easily leave the Indians too scattered to oppose their enemies effectively. The Indians' tactics, moreover, could be countered.

Little Turtle urged the Indians to avoid a large battle and instead to attack the supply convoys upon which the advancing Americans would depend. When such attacks failed to stop Wayne from reaching the Maumee, he tried to persuade the Indians to make peace. When he failed, he refused to serve further as a commander beyond leading the Miami at the battle.

The other Indian commanders decided to await Wayne's army at Fallen Timbers. As at Wabash, they would surround the Americans. The Americans then would fire their massed muskets and artillery to no effect, suffer large casualties in fruitless dragoon and bayonet charges, and ultimately flee from the field. The confident Indian commanders did not think it necessary to analyze how Wayne might respond to such a plan. "The Indians had been so successful against St. Clair," remembered the Shawnee Jonathan Alder, "that they made no other plans but that they were going to have the same results with General Wayne. But it turned out to be very different."

Little Turtle died in 1812 in Fort Wayne, Indiana, at the house of his daughter Manwangopatti and son-in-law William Wells. His remains, accidentally disinterred in 1912, were recognized by this sword given to him by George Washington when Little Turtle visited Philadelphia in 1796. (Courtesy of the Allen County-Fort Wayne Historical Society)

THE FALLEN TIMBERS CAMPAIGN

FROM LEGIONVILLE TO FORT GREENEVILLE

On April 30, 1793, Wayne's ornamented barge *The Federal* left Legionville. Thirty large flatboats, each displaying unit flags, followed at 100yds intervals. Swept by the flooded Ohio, they went downstream at twice the usual speed for river traffic. Ten-year-old Ezra Ferris, who saw them arrive in Cincinnati on May 5, remembered decades later how Wayne's army was "hailed with joy, and the people now felt as though they were secure."

The Americans camped just west of Cincinnati, on the only suitable site. The story of the stable owner Thomas Hobson, who offered his customers only one horse, gave the army's first camp its name. At Hobson's Choice, Wayne immediately began preparing for the army's advance.

Wayne and his Quartermaster General, John O'Hara, conferred with the army's chief contractor Robert Elliott, the brother of McKee's assistant Matthew Elliott, on the massive logistical operation to come. Convoys of wagons and packhorses would transport food and other supplies to the forwardmost American position, Fort Jefferson. On May 24, he sent McMahon and 100 riflemen to reinforce the distant outpost.

St. Clair's Trace led 75 miles north to Fort Jefferson. The 15ft-wide road, Wayne concluded, was too primitive to carry the wagon traffic his campaign would require. He ordered Lt. Col. David Strong to build a 44ft-wide road as far as Fort Jefferson. Sometimes following St. Clair's straight path and sometimes deviating onto easier ground, 500 men then built Strong's Road, the first portion of what would be remembered as Wayne's Trace.

The American commander soon received news that the Chickasaws in northern Mississippi were willing to send aid for his campaign. He dispatched Lt. William Clark and a party down the Ohio. Clark, who was to evade detection by the Spanish on the Mississippi, was to return with Chickasaw warriors who could serve as scouts.

By May 25, the three American peace commissioners had arrived at Fort Niagara. The Indians, they were told, had assembled at the foot of the Miami Rapids, not Sandusky. They must wait for word on whether the Indians would receive them.

At Hobson's Choice, continuing pleas for help from settlers interrupted Wayne's planning. On June 5, Indians killed a man and wounded another near Fort Randolph. On June 6, 7, and 17, they attacked soldiers and stole horses near Fort Hamilton. In July, Kentuckians led by Simon Kenton ambushed Indian raiders at the mouth of Holt's Creek on the Ohio, killing six. Disputes also distracted the American commander. Those between soldiers and settlers, he announced, would be resolved in the courts. "Civil law," he said, "is paramount to the military – a principle that shall ever be supported." There also was discord within the army. Wilkinson, who had greeted Wayne's arrival with profuse expressions of delight, soon was at odds with his commander. The two men, Lt. Col. John Hamtramck wrote to another officer, "after being for some time great friends, have declared war."

Wayne concluded the hostilities by sending Wilkinson to command distant Fort Jefferson. Wilkinson's exile, however, did not end Wayne's problems. The American commander received disturbing reports of unexpected resignations, insults that ended in duels, and bold acts of insubordination by junior officers. He discreetly began assembling a network of trusted officers who could provide information on such incidents.

On July 5, 50 Indians arrived for preliminary negotiations with the American commissioners. At Navy Hall in Newark, the Americans met with Simcoe, Brant, and the Indians. Wayne had built new roads, reinforced his forts, and accumulated supplies for war, the furious Indians said. Threatening the Americans, they demanded that such actions be halted. Wayne's activities, the frightened commissioners wrote to Knox on July 10, were endangering their lives.

As Wayne forwarded soldiers and supplies to Fort Jefferson, he waited impatiently for the letter from the commissioners that would authorize his advance. Wells, who had volunteered to serve as an American scout, then made an unexpected offer. He would go to the Indian council himself and return with accurate information on the Indians' intentions. On July 10, Wells reached the foot of the Maumee Rapids and blended in among the more than 2,000 Indians gathered there.

On July 14, the American commissioners were allowed to sail west. They traveled, however, not to the foot of the Maumee Rapids, but to Matthew Elliott's house overlooking the Detroit River. There, they were told, they would learn whether the Indians would receive them. As the American

This painting by Rudolph Tschudi depicts Cincinnati in 1800, when its population had grown to about 800. Fort Washington is shown in the upper right. Hobson's Choice was beyond the scene to the left. (Cincinnati Museum Center)

This 1792–93 portrait by Charles Willson Peale depicts Timothy Pickering, one of the three American peace commissioners. In 1795, he would succeed Henry Knox as Secretary of War. (Independence National Historical Park)

commissioners waited, Genêt established a base for his revolutionary activities in New York. He recruited for service as French consuls émigrés like the famous botanist André Michaux. In dozens of eastern cities, Americans inspired by Genêt organized Democratic-Republican societies modeled on the Jacobin Club, where Parisians debated the course of the French Revolution. On town greens across the country, sympathizers erected liberty poles, symbols of opposition to aristocracy and government restrictions on freedom. The French minister began openly calling for a new American government. The US House of Representatives, Genêt announced, was the only part of the American federal government actually elected by the people. It alone should appoint leaders to rule the United States. Genêt also completed his plans for war, which would commence in 1794. In the south, 1,500 Georgia frontiersmen would capture Spanish Florida. Across the Appalachians, 2,000 Virginia, North Carolina, and Tennessee frontiersman would join 2,000 Kentuckians. As the French Revolutionary Legion on the Mississippi, they would conquer Spanish Louisiana. On July 15, Michaux and two French artillery officers went west to Kentucky with a commission for Clark, who would lead the western army as a French major-general.

On July 29, 50 Indians arrived at Elliott's house. As they scowled through the windows, Elliott assured the commissioners that they were safe as long as they remained inside. Simon Girty, who acted as translator for the Indian negotiators, angrily demanded on August 1 that the Americans abandon their forts and settlements beyond the Ohio River. When the commissioners rejected the ultimatum, he told them that they would learn within two weeks a final decision by the Indians on war or peace.

The year before his election as US president in 1840, William Henry Harrison would write *A Discourse on the Origins of the Aborigines of the Ohio Valley*, one of the first works on the prehistoric Ohio 'Moundbuilders'. While earlier serving as governor of the Indiana Territory, he built this 1804 house in Vincennes, now a museum devoted to his life. (Grouseland Foundation, Vincennes, Ind.)

At Hobson's Choice, Lt. William Henry Harrison diverted his impatient commander with tours of the massive earthworks in the area, left by the prehistoric Ohio "Moundbuilders." On August 8, however, new orders arrived. Knox, who had received the commissioners' July 10 letter, ordered Wayne to preserve "the truce." He must withdraw any soldiers at the advanced Ohio forts "exceeding their usual garrisons" and stop accumulating supplies there. There was no truce, the infuriated Wayne replied, enclosing with his response copies of officers' reports of recent Indian attacks. In an exasperated postscript, he added that he had just received another such report "The woods and roads are infested by savages," he wrote, "Would to God that my hands were untied."

On August 16, two Wyandots arrived at Elliott's house with a letter written in English. The American settlers, it said, must abandon their homes beyond the Ohio River. The American government, it added, should compensate them with the money it had planned to pay the Indians for their land. "No person having knowledge of the Indians and their modes of expression," the astonished American interpreter John Heckewelder told the commissioners, "would believe it an Indian speech." The author had been British Capt. Joseph Bunbury of the 5th Regiment of Foot. The peace commissioners then returned to American territory. On August 23, they dispatched their letter to Wayne by multiple messengers. On the same day, Lt. William Clark returned from his mission to Mississippi with the Chickasaw chief James Underwood and eight warriors. On September 11, the commissioners' August 23 letter reached Hobson's Choice. Wayne quickly found the words that authorized an advance. "Tho we did not effect a peace, yet we hope that good may hereafter arise from our mission," the letter said.

This copy of the letter authorizing Wayne's advance survives in the US National Archives. (Author's collection)

Little time remained for a campaign in 1793. Wayne, who had 2,600 men ready to go forward, immediately sent a courier to Scott, asking him to bring 1,500 Kentucky horsemen to Fort Jefferson. On September 12, he ordered that Strong's Road be extended as far as Greenville Creek. When Wayne's letter reached Scott on September 13, Scott immediately began recruiting volunteers. Kenton and others, who would serve as captains, feverishly tried to find men willing to serve in a campaign that would last into winter.

On the same day Wayne's letter reached Scott, Michaux arrived in Lexington to begin organizing Genêt's western army. From Kentucky Governor Isaac Shelby, who had led the Americans to victory at King's Mountain in 1780, he received a warm welcome. Washington, who had tried to ignore Genêt's activities, was at last forced to act. Secretary of State Thomas Jefferson dispatched a letter to Paris. If the French government did not replace Genêt, Jefferson wrote, the United States would terminate diplomatic relations with France.

On September 16, as Michaux was meeting with Clark in Louisville, Wells reported to Wayne what had happened at the Indian council. The Indian leaders, he said, had met with McKee and Girty at a council house near McKee's trading post. They had three times decided to ask the Americans to come to the council, but each time McKee had dissuaded them. The Indians at the council, Wells also reported, had included many Iroquois and even southern Cherokees, Creeks, Chickasaws, and Choctaws. There would be a big war the following year, the Indians had said. The British and Iroquois would attack the Americans in New York. The British and Ohio Indians would attack on the Ohio River frontier. The Spanish and the southern Indians, after killing the pro-American Chickasaw and Choctaw leaders, would attack Georgia and the Southwest Territory.

Wells's report left Wayne eager to go forward as soon as possible. Disaster, however, then struck the Americans. An outbreak of influenza erupted at Hobson's Choice. Smallpox arrived from Fort Harmar. A puzzled O'Hara then reported that the army lacked supplies for an advance. Knox's August 8 order had wrought chaos in the army's logistical planning. But that did not explain what Wayne's Quartermaster General had discovered. The stores at the advanced forts contained only a quarter of the flour that should be there. Elliott and the contractors, moreover, had no explanation for the deficit. Suffering from gout and stricken by influenza, Wayne tried to obtain more supplies for the campaign. He ordered purchase of all available flour.

This statue of Simon Kenton, designed by John Quincy Adams Ward and completed by Mike Major, stands near the grave of the great frontiersman in Urbana, Ohio. (Photograph by Dale Benington)

He detached hundreds of the army's horses for use in carrying the flour and pulling supply wagons forward.

By October 7, Wayne and O'Hara had accumulated sufficient food to advance. The American army then marched 10 miles up Strong's Road to its second camp. From October 8 through 12, the army continued forward, stopping at its third through seventh camps. On October 13, it reached Greenville Creek. There, at its eighth camp, it would await Scott's Kentuckians.

As the Americans had marched north, the Ottawa leader Little Otter had led a party of 40 Indians south. On October 16, while patrolling near the army's eighth camp, Cornet William Blue and 24 dragoons saw two Indians. After Blue and three horsemen had pursued them 100yds, four concealed Indians killed two of Blue's men. The retreating dragoon commander then found that the remainder of his force had fled. Infuriated by Blue's report, Wayne had his officers read aloud to each company in the army an order that any man fleeing from battle would be shot.

That night, a ten-wagon convoy advancing to Wayne's eighth camp halted a mile north of the fifth camp. There, 20 civilian drivers and 90 riflemen and dragoons, led by Lt. John Lowry, camped on what would be called Lowry Run. At dawn on October 17, Little Otter's warriors attacked. After killing Lowry and 15 men, and capturing another ten, they moved further south. On October 19, they attacked White's Station, where they killed a man and two children.

The Ohio River to Greenville creek

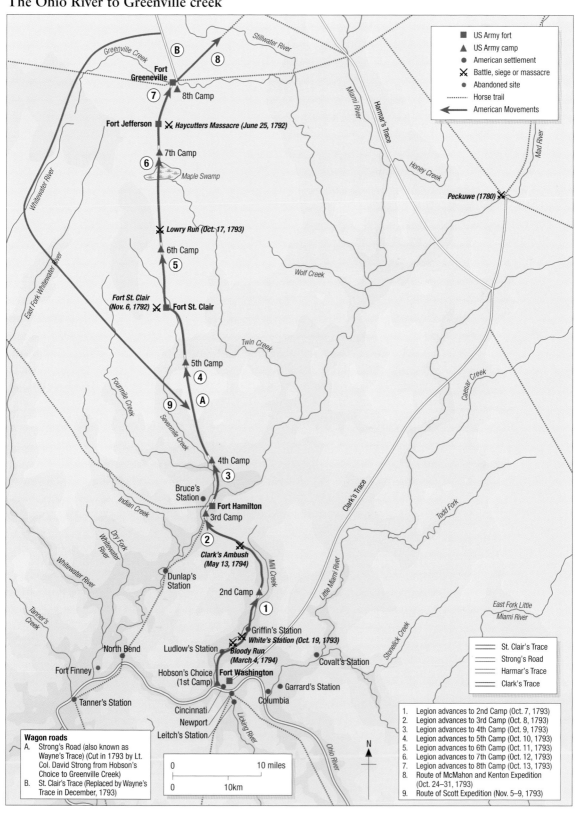

Legend:
- ■ US Army fort
- ▲ US Army camp
- ● American settlement
- ✕ Battle, siege or massacre
- ● Abandoned site
- ⋯⋯ Horse trail
- ← American Movements

Greenville Creek

Stillwater River

Ⓑ

Ⓐ

Fort Greeneville ▲ 8th Camp
⑦

Miami River

Harmar's Trace

Mad River

Fort Jefferson ■ ✕ *Haycutters Massacre (June 25, 1792)*

Whitewater River

⑥ ▲ 7th Camp

Honey Creek

Maple Swamp

Peckuwe (1780) ✕

East Fork Whitewater River

✕ *Lowry Run (Oct. 17, 1793)*

▲ 6th Camp
⑤

Wolf Creek

Fort St. Clair *(Nov. 6, 1792)* ✕ ■ **Fort St. Clair**

Twin Creek

Caesar Creek

Fourmile Creek

▲ 5th Camp
④
Ⓐ

⑨

Sevenmile Creek

Clark's Trace

Todd Fork

Indian Creek

▲ 4th Camp
③

Bruce's Station ●

Fort Hamilton ■
3rd Camp

②

Clark's Ambush (May 13, 1794) ✕

Dry Fork Whitewater River

Dunlap's Station ●

Whitewater River

Little Miami River

2nd Camp ▲
①

Mill Creek

East Fork Little Miami River

Tanner's Creek

Griffin's Station ●
✕✕ *White's Station (Oct. 19, 1793)*
Ludlow's Station ● *Bloody Run (March 4, 1794)*

Stonelick Creek

North Bend ●

Fort Finney ●

Hobson's Choice (1st Camp) **Fort Washington** ■

Covalt's Station ●

Tanner's Station ●

Cincinnati
Newport
Leitch's Station

Columbia
● **Garrard's Station**

Licking River

Ohio River

N

Wagon roads
A. Strong's Road (also known as Wayne's Trace) (Cut in 1793 by Lt. Col. David Strong from Hobson's Choice to Greenville Creek)
B. St. Clair's Trace (Replaced by Wayne's Trace in December, 1793)

0 ——————— 10 miles
0 ——————— 10km

	St. Clair's Trace
	Strong's Road
	Harmar's Trace
	Clark's Trace

1. Legion advances to 2nd Camp (Oct. 7, 1793)
2. Legion advances to 3rd Camp (Oct. 8, 1793)
3. Legion advances to 4th Camp (Oct. 9, 1793)
4. Legion advances to 5th Camp (Oct. 10, 1793)
5. Legion advances to 6th Camp (Oct. 11, 1793)
6. Legion advances to 7th Camp (Oct. 12, 1793)
7. Legion advances to 8th Camp (Oct. 13, 1793)
8. Route of McMahon and Kenton Expedition (Oct. 24–31, 1793)
9. Route of Scott Expedition (Nov. 5–9, 1793)

The photograph shows an area of the Andrew S. Janicki model of Fort Greeneville displayed at the Garst Museum in Greenville, Ohio. The area includes Wayne's headquarters (bottom left), staff quarters (bottom right), and officers' gardens (bottom center), below the fortified "Citadel," where the artillery and munitions were guarded. (Author's photograph)

On October 21, Scott arrived at Wayne's eighth camp with 500 volunteer horsemen, and another 500 Kentuckians he had been forced to draft. Before advancing, Wayne ordered a reconnaissance in strength. On October 24, Kenton and 100 horsemen, and McMahon and 47 Legion riflemen, went up an Indian trail toward abandoned Loramie's Trading Post. That night the weather turned bad. First came the season's first heavy snow and then a hard frost. Days of freezing rain followed.

As Kenton's and McMahon's men moved north through abandoned Girty's Town and Tawa Town, and down the Auglaize, Wayne weighed whether to go forward when they returned. His men's enlistment terms would begin expiring the following spring. The stakes of his mission, however, were too high to risk failure. On October 31, he convened a council of his senior officers. All agreed that there was too little time and too little food for a campaign.

When Kenton and McMahon returned, the Kentuckians departed. On November 5, Scott's 500 volunteers commenced a brief expedition to the Whitewater River. After four days of fruitless searching for Indians, they then followed Scott's draftees back to Kentucky. The American commander, however, would not retreat from Greenville Creek. On November 6, his soldiers began fortifying a permanent, 55-acre camp, which Wayne called Greene Ville. Named for his deceased friend Maj. Gen. Nathanael Greene, or perhaps Greene's widow, it would be remembered as Fort Greeneville. On November 13, Wayne sent Wilkinson and 500 men to escort a large convoy with provisions for winter. He then sent the army's dragoons and supply horses to a winter camp near Lexington, which the horsemen named Bellerephontia.

The failure of Wayne's contractors to provide supplies remained unexplained. So did the pattern of discord within the army that had emerged after its arrival at Hobson's Choice. On November 15, the American commander sent to Knox a report on the results of his investigation. With an innocuous report on the army's condition, Wayne sent a more candid communication marked "Private and Confidential." "The same baneful leaven which has been and is yet fermenting in the Atlantic states," he wrote

to Knox "has also been fermenting in this Legion, from the moment of my first landing at Hobson's Choice… The most visible and acting person is a Major Cushing, who is a very artful and seditious man."

There was, however, something deeper, Wayne reported, something that he had not yet found. Those responsible for the flour shortage, he wrote, "expected that I should be compelled to retreat, for want of supplies." The following spring, he predicted, "the next attempt will be to default my advance." But Genêt's partisans had no reason to obstruct an American campaign against the Indians. His army, Wayne wrote, apparently was threatened "by a many headed monster." Still waiting for a French response to his complaints about Genêt, Washington at last took direct action. On December 5, he addressed Congress. The French minister, Washington announced, was attempting "to excite discord and distrust, between our citizens and those whom they have entrusted with their government, between the different branches of our government, between our nation and his." Those attempts, he said, now would be suppressed. As 1793 approached its end, Wayne was uncertain what operations he would be called upon to undertake in 1794. He had arrived at Hobson's Choice to fight the Ohio Indians. The British, the Iroquois, the Spanish, the southern Indians, and the French Revolutionary Legion, however, were all now potential enemies. There also were still hidden adversaries.

Wayne expanded his efforts to discover their identities and plans. Wells and a company of scouts were to capture prisoners with knowledge of British agents and activities. Major John Belli, Wayne's Deputy Quartermaster, was to organize a network of sources to provide intelligence on activities in Kentucky. The careful American commander also tried to ensure that his secret enemies would not find again an area in which his army was vulnerable. O'Hara carefully specified what the contractors were to do in 1794. To be certain that they could provide the army's 4,125 daily rations, they were to accumulate a 270,000-ration reserve. To insure that they would have 600 packhorses for convoys, they were to maintain ready for use an additional 250.

Wayne also tried to foresee what new actions his hidden adversaries might take. A potential area of operations, Wayne thought, might be Philadelphia. He dispatched Posey, whom Washington considered almost a son, and Scott to the national capital to shape the field on which any battle there would be fought.

FROM FORT GREENEVILLE TO FORT RECOVERY

The American commander was determined to end 1793 with a significant accomplishment. Twenty-four miles up St. Clair's Trace lay the field of the battle of the Wabash. On December 23, Wayne led 300 men to the site, widening the road as they went. On Christmas Day, they found the remains of St. Clair's army. "When we went to lay down in our tents at night," remembered Pvt. George Will, "we had to scrape the bones together and carry them out to make our beds." There the Americans began building a symbol of national resolve, which Wayne named Fort Recovery.

Wayne also ordered aggressive reconnaissance operations northeast of Fort Greeneville. On January 1, 1794, the frontiersman Joseph Collins and 14 of Eaton's Green Mountain Boys encountered a larger party of Indians a mile south of Girty's Town. Three of the Americans were killed and two wounded at Collins's Fight. When Eaton led a larger force back to the battlefield, they found seven Indian bodies still there.

Wayne then ordered Capt. Asa Hartshorne to build a road as far as the site. On January 6, Hartshorne's men began felling trees along the Indian path to Loramie's Trading Post. From there, they improved Harmar's Trace as far as Girty's Town. On January 11, two Indian warriors appeared at Fort Greeneville carrying a white flag. One was George White Eyes, son of the famous chief White Eyes, who had led the pro-American Delaware during the Revolutionary War. The Delaware warrior had returned to Ohio in 1789, shortly before graduating from Princeton. The Indians at the Glaize, George White Eyes said, wanted peace. If so, Wayne replied, they should prove it by delivering to Fort Recovery by February 14 their American prisoners. Three days later, Indians attacked a wagon convoy 2 miles south of Fort Hamilton, killing one American and capturing two.

This 1815 portrait by Rembrandt Peale depicts Capt. William Eaton. In 1805, he would lead a force of US Marines and Arab allies to a victory over the army of the Pasha of Tripoli. the battle is commemorated in the famous line of the Marines' Hymn "to the shores of Tripoli." (Collection of Maryland State Archives, MSA SC 4680-10-0082)

As the winter days passed at Fort Greeneville, couriers arrived with news from Wayne's network of intelligence agents. When George White Eyes had returned to the Glaize, Indians captured by Wells disclosed, Matthew Elliott and Girty had persuaded the Indians there not to make peace. McKee, moreover, had promised to assemble at the Glaize in the spring a large Indian army to fight the Americans.

From his agents in Kentucky, Wayne learned what had caused the food supply failure. Wilkinson had organized a conspiracy that included US Army officers, army contractors and powerful political figures. Its object was to keep an American army led by Wayne from reaching the Maumee. Reports from his agents provided ever more information about the conspirators and their plans. On the day George White Eyes visited Fort Greeneville, Wayne's agent Cornet William Blue wrote from Bellerephontia. Lieutenant Campbell Smith, he reported, was a Wilkinson partisan. Certain congressmen, he had also learned, were trying to persuade Washington to appoint Wilkinson to replace Wayne.

Each new courier brought more information about the difficult situation Wayne would face in 1794. On January 25, Clark placed a recruiting advertisement in Cincinnati's new newspaper, the *Centinel of the Northwest Territory*. His French Revolutionary Legion, it said, would invade Spanish Louisiana the following summer. Those who enlisted would receive large land grants and "all lawful plunder."

After returning from London, Dorchester told a delegation of Iroquois on February 10 that Britain would probably declare war against the United States. "I shall not be surprised if we are at war with them in the course of the present year," he said, "I believe our patience is almost exhausted." Dorchester's speech alarmed the American government in Philadelphia. To avoid a war, Washington decided to send a special emissary to London. Chief Justice John Jay, who had with Benjamin Franklin and John Adams negotiated the original Treaty of Paris, agreed to go.

On February 17, Dorchester ordered Simcoe to build an advanced fort on the Maumee to protect Detroit. When George Hammond, the British minister to the United States, learned of the order, he protested. It would be an act of war, he wrote to London, to build a fort on what Britain acknowledged to be American territory.

On February 22, a new French minister arrived in Philadelphia to replace Genêt. Jean-Antoine-Joseph Fauchet, who brought with him a warrant for his predecessor's arrest, agreed to stop the military adventures that Genêt had planned. On March 4, Fauchet issued an order canceling Clark's expedition. On the same day, Indians attacked a packhorse convoy near White's Station. At Bloody Run, they killed two and wounded one.

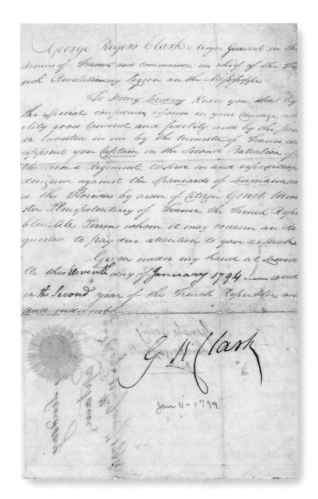

On January 11, 1794, George Rogers Clark, as "major general in the armies of France," issued to Henry Lindsay, one of the first settlers of Cincinnati, this commission as a captain in the "French Revolutionary Legion on the Mississippi." (Courtesy of the Special Collections Research Center, University of Chicago Library)

Despite Fauchet's action, Clark continued to prepare for his campaign. Desperate to avoid the war with Spain that Clark's invasion would provoke, the Washington administration asked Arthur St. Clair, the Governor of the Northwest Territory, and Shelby, the Governor of Kentucky, to stop the recruiting for Clark's army. When Shelby refused, Washington announced on March 24 that the federal government would take action against any men who joined Clark's expedition.

On March 31, Knox ordered Wayne to build a fort on the Ohio River at the site of old French Fort Massac. What the Americans would call Fort Massac would guard Kentucky from a Spanish invasion. The fort's guns, Knox also directed, were to be used on Clark's army if it attempted to descend the river.

Knox's March 31 letter revealed how well Posey and Scott had performed their assignments in Philadelphia. Washington, it said, approved of Wayne's actions as commander and had the highest confidence in him. In a separate letter, marked "Private and Confidential," Wayne learned how important their work had been. Several congressmen, Knox wrote, had begun spreading defamatory rumors about Wayne's conduct in Ohio. Washington's expression of confidence in him, Knox added, should be made public to discredit "the disorganizers be they who they may be." The conspirators then intensified their attack. On April 4, Wilkinson wrote directly to Washington and Knox

At the time of his appointment as Quartermaster General, James O'Hara lived in this cabin, which survives in Pittsburgh's Schenley Park. He later became a prominent Pittsburgh merchant and banker. (Courtesy of Pittsburgh History and Landmarks Foundation)

accusing his commander of incompetence and corruption. On April 13, an anonymous officer sent to the *Centinel* a report with similar accusations, which he entitled "Stubborn Facts." The *Centinel* refused to publish the report. On April 16, however, "Stubborn Facts" appeared in a Virginia paper, the *Martinsburg Gazette*, and was widely reprinted in other newspapers.

As Jay sailed to London in search of peace, Simcoe prepared for war. After conferring at Detroit with Col. Richard England, commander of the 24th Regiment of Foot, he sailed south. On April 10, he began to build on the Maumee what would be called Fort Miamis. On April 18, Maj. William Campbell arrived with a garrison of three companies of the 24th and 50 artillerymen with eight guns. Soon, Simcoe told the Ohio Indian chiefs, Ojibwe, Potawatomi, Ottawa, and Wyandot warriors would arrive from Michigan and Canada, and also Iroquois led by Joseph Brant.

Despite the threats posed by the Spanish and Clark's French Revolutionary Legion, Wayne began preparing for an advance against the Indians in July. On April 19, Wells's scouts ambushed ten warriors on the St. Marys River, wounding several. On April 24, Indians attacked American settlements on Blennerhasset Island, killing three and capturing four.

O'Hara, who carefully monitored the contractors' activities, repeatedly complained to Robert Elliott that supplies for the July campaign were not being delivered on schedule. His complaints, he finally told Wayne on May 1, were being treated with "contempt." The American commander then ordered McMahon to buy all available cattle, flour, and horses. Whatever the cost, Wayne wrote to Elliott, the contractors would pay it. He then added to his threat a chilling comment. "Facts," he wrote, "are stubborn things." Facing financial ruin or worse, the frightened contractors immediately began delivering supplies. Even with their cooperation, however, the logistical operation was difficult. On May 13, 60 Delaware and Shawnee attacked a 700-horse convoy moving toward Fort Hamilton at Clark's Ambush. Before Lt. William Clark's 60 infantrymen and 20 dragoons drove them off, they killed eight and wounded two Americans, and took 40 horses.

On May 29, Wayne received welcome reinforcements. Underwood returned with about 60 Chickasaws. The famous Tennessee frontiersman James Robertson, the founder of Nashville, arrived with 45 Choctaws. They brought with them, however, bad news. Five large Spanish gunboats, each with 60 men, had sailed up the Mississippi to the mouth of the Ohio. Wayne ordered Capt. Thomas Doyle to take an infantry company and four guns to garrison new Fort Massac. More bad news followed. Wells's scouts reported to Wayne that Simcoe was building Fort Miamis. "I am placed in a very delicate and disagreeable situation," the American commander wrote to Knox on May 30, "the very quarter which I wished to strike at, i.e., the centre of the hostile tribes – the British are now in possession of." On the same day, Indians believed to be Senecas attacked boats on the Allegheny River, killing four Americans and wounding two. The Iroquois tribes, it appeared, were likely to join the Ohio Indians.

This 1807–08 portrait by Charles Willson Peale depicts Lt. William Clark. (Independence National Historical Park)

To battle the growing number of potential American enemies, moreover, Wayne no longer had the army that had arrived at Hobson's Choice the year before. After two years of service many of his best officers had resigned, including Putnam, Posey, and Capt. Henry Carberry, who had saved the US Army from complete annihilation at Wabash. Others, like Eaton, had been sent on recruiting missions to restore the army's depleted ranks.

The expiration of his soldiers' two-year enlistment terms had left many of his three-company regular infantry battalions themselves the size of companies. In July, Scott would bring Kentucky horsemen for the campaign. How many would arrive, however, was uncertain. Wilkinson and his conspirators also remained active. He would keep Wilkinson with the advancing army in command of one of its two wings, Wayne decided, but closely watched. He appointed two loyal officers, Capt. Jacob Kingsbury and Capt. William Peters, to lead the two sublegions under Wilkinson's command. He then acted to diminish a risk that Wilkinson's presence would create. On June 8, Wayne announced that, if he were killed or incapacitated during the campaign, Scott would succeed him as American commander

This partial reconstruction of Fort Recovery is at the Fort Recovery State Museum in Fort Recovery, Ohio. (Photograph by John Stanton)

This portrait by an unknown artist depicts Thomas McKee. (Windsor's Community Museum 1976.4).

By June 16, McKee had gathered about 1,600 Indian warriors at the Glaize, including Ojibwe, Potawatomi, Ottawa, and Wyandots from Michigan and Canada. The Indian commanders decided to use the huge force, the largest Indian army yet assembled, to attack Wayne's convoys. They might even be able to capture Fort Recovery. In 1791, St. Clair had abandoned eight pieces of artillery at Wabash, which the Indians had left buried on the battlefield. If the Indians could recover the guns, they could, with British aid, use them to reduce the fort.

The Indian army, which would have to sustain itself by hunting, was too large to advance in a single body. About 1,200 would go forward first, hunting east of the Auglaize River. Another 400, led by Buckongahelas, would await reinforcements and then advance through an area west of the river. On June 19, the first 1,200 went forward in 12 widely dispersed columns. Alexander McKee and his son Thomas, Matthew Elliott, Simon Girty, and Canadian volunteers dressed as Indians accompanied them. A British captain, sergeant, and six artillerymen brought the expertise and munitions needed to operate St. Clair's guns.

On June 26, Wayne sent the Chickasaws and Choctaws forward as scouts. Wearing yellow ribbons to distinguish them from the Ohio Indians, Underwood and the Chickasaws moved north above Fort Recovery, while Roberson's Choctaws, with Wells and ten scouts, went up Hartshorne's Road. On June 27, 20 Ojibwes and Ottawas ambushed four Choctaws near Girty's Town, killing one. On June 28, the Choctaws returned to Fort Greeneville, and reported that a large Indian army was moving south.

Fort Recovery consisted of two structures, surrounded by cleared ground for 200 yards in every direction. The fort itself had four blockhouses connected by 15ft-high stockade walls. A fifth, isolated, blockhouse stood nearby on the Wabash River. Captain Alexander Gibson, the fort commandant, had a substantial garrison to protect the forwardmost American outpost. His rifle company and Capt. Russell Bissell's infantry company, led in Bissell's absence by Lt. Samuel Drake, defended the fort. A corporal and six privates guarded the blockhouse. Gibson also had 25 artillerymen and seven guns. During the prior six months, his soldiers had unearthed two 6lb guns, two 3lb guns, and a small carronade abandoned at

Captured at the age of nine in 1782 in Virginia, Jonathan Alder fought at Fort Recovery as an adopted Shawnee. In this 1806 cabin, now at the Madison County (Ohio) Historical Society, he wrote his *A History of Jonathan Alder*, an account of his life in early Ohio. (Author's photograph)

Wabash. The five recovered guns and two additional howitzers now were aimed through embrasures on the ground floors of the fort's blockhouses.

On June 29, Indian scouts reported that an American convoy was approaching Fort Recovery. Scattering the Chickasaws along the St. Marys River, the Indians moved southwest to attack it. That evening, the 360-horse convoy camped outside the fort. Its guard, led by McMahon, consisted of 50 dragoons commanded by Capt. James Taylor and 90 riflemen led by Capt. Asa Hartshorne. Just before dawn on June 30, Underwood and a small party of Chickasaws reached Fort Recovery. The Chickasaw chief, who spoke no English, frantically tried to communicate the situation he had raced to report. "All we could understand from him," Gibson remembered, "was that he had seen a great many tracks and heard much firing." As McMahon's convoy guard finished their breakfasts, the horsemasters began leading their packhorses down the trace to Fort Greeneville. When they were 200yds into the woods, the Indians attacked. At the sound of gunfire, McMahon, with Taylor and his dragoons, rode to protect them. Hartshorne followed, with rifle platoons on the horsemen's flanks.

Shots soon killed McMahon and wounded Taylor and Hartshorne. The dragoons retreated to the blockhouse on the Wabash, where they tried to regroup. The Indians then surrounded Hartshorne's riflemen. The wounded American captain ordered his men to leave him and fight their way back to the fort. Indians led by Thomas McKee then demanded that Hartshorne surrender. Hopping on one leg, the American captain instead used his espontoon to knock McKee off his horse before the Indians killed and scalped him.

Gibson sent Drake and 20 infantrymen to clear a path for the fleeing riflemen. As the Indians fell back from their bayonets, a shot wounded Drake. As he and the surviving infantrymen, riflemen, and horsemasters retreated through the clearing back to the fort, the Indians attacked the dragoons near the blockhouse. Abandoning their horses, the dragoons fled to the fort. "The Indians," the Shawnee Jonathan Alder recalled, "run them so close that there was, I reckon, as many as fifty horses that the whites sprung off of, and got into the fort as best they could." The Indians, Alder said, then "surrounded the garrison, and fired from every direction, and advanced as far as they could find stumps and trees to cover them." "Musket balls," remembered Isaac Paxton of Gibson's rifle company, "were heard continually striking against the pickets and logs of the blockhouses, and whizzing over the heads of those in the garrison." But the Indians had no targets. An Indian commander, Alder remembered, told him to "Shoot those holes in the fort. You might kill a man."

The Indians had killed or wounded dozens of Americans and captured more than 300 horses. But they wanted a victory worthy of such a large army – the capture of the fort. The puzzled Americans saw parties examining portions of the field that had no apparent significance. But the Indians could find none of the three guns that remained buried. Despite the failure, they would not abandon the field. Determined to achieve their goal, they tried to storm the American stronghold. "They assailed the fort with great fury," remembered Paxton, "rushing up to within less than fifty yards of it, some of them carrying axes and hatchets for the purpose of cutting down the pickets." The fort, however, bristled with weapons. Within its walls about 120 riflemen and seven guns had a clear field of fire.

This portrait by Chester Harding, painted about 1820, depicts Brand Ballard, who led a company in Maj. Aquila Whitaker's battalion. (Courtesy of the Filson Historical Society, Louisville, Ky.)

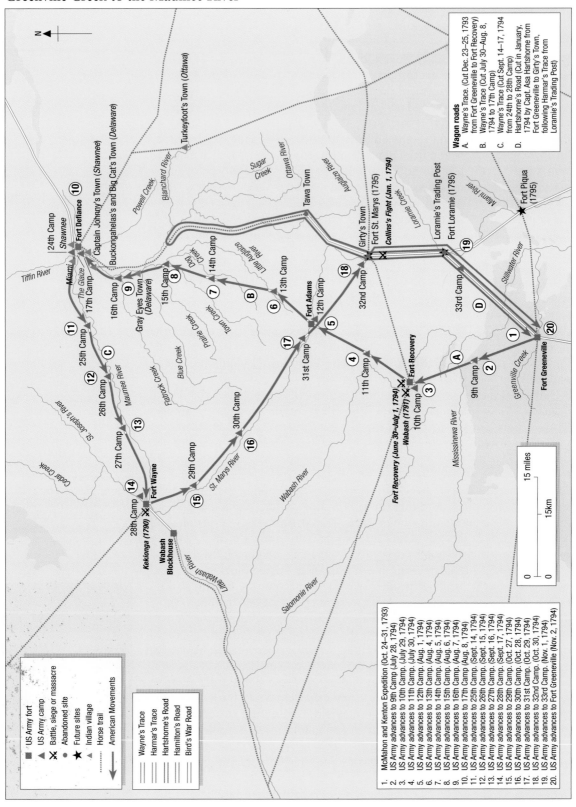

Wagon roads

A. Wayne's Trace. (Cut Dec. 23–25, 1793 from Fort Greeneville to Fort Recovery)
B. Wayne's Trace (Cut July 30–Aug. 8, 1794 to 17th Camp)
C. Wayne's Trace (Cut Sept. 14–17, 1794 from 24th to 28th Camp)
D. Hartshorne's Road (Cut in January, 1794 by Capt. Asa Hartshorne from Fort Greeneville to Girty's Town, following Harmar's Trace from Loramie's Trading Post)

Legend (US Army symbols):
- ■ US Army fort
- ▲ US Army camp
- ✕ Battle, siege or massacre
- ● Abandoned site
- ○ Future sites
- ★ Indian village
- ⋯ Horse trail
- → American Movements

Wagon roads (map lines):
- Wayne's Trace
- Harmar's Trace
- Hartshorne's Road
- Hamilton's Road
- Bird's War Road

1. McMahon and Kenton Expedition (Oct. 24–31, 1793)
2. US Army advances to 9th Camp (July 28, 1794)
3. US Army advances to 10th Camp. (July 29, 1794)
4. US Army advances to 11th Camp. (July 30, 1794)
5. US Army advances to 12th Camp. (Aug. 1, 1794)
6. US Army advances to 13th Camp. (Aug. 4, 1794)
7. US Army advances to 14th Camp. (Aug. 5, 1794)
8. US Army advances to 15th Camp. (Aug. 6, 1794)
9. US Army advances to 16th Camp. (Aug. 7, 1794)
10. US Army advances to 17th Camp (Aug. 8, 1794)
11. US Army advances to 25th Camp. (Sept. 14, 1794)
12. US Army advances to 26th Camp. (Sept. 15, 1794)
13. US Army advances to 27th Camp. (Sept. 16, 1794)
14. US Army advances to 28th Camp. (Sept. 17, 1794)
15. US Army advances to 29th Camp. (Oct. 27, 1794)
16. US Army advances to 30th Camp. (Oct. 28, 1794)
17. US Army advances to 31st Camp. (Oct. 29, 1794)
18. US Army advances to 32nd Camp. (Oct. 30, 1794)
19. US Army advances to 33rd Camp. (Nov. 1, 1794)
20. US Army advances to Fort Greeneville (Nov. 2, 1794)

15 miles
15km

As rifle balls found their targets and scythes of canister shot cut through sections of the clearing, the Indians fled back to the woods. The Americans then used their artillery to fire shells above the trees. Explosions in midair at a distance of about 400yds rained balls and shell fragments down on the Indians. "I began to feel pretty badly scared," Alder recalled, "I thought that we were surrounded." The fear was justified among the Ojibwes. The evening before, rumors had spread among the Indians that late-arriving Ojibwes had abused and terrorized Shawnee women and children at the Glaize. Now Underwood's Chickasaws had begun killing Ojibwe warriors at the rear of their section of the Indian line. When the Ojibwe found warriors who had been scalped, they concluded that vengeful Shawnee had taken the hair.

Despite Shawnee denials that they had attacked their allies, the unhappy Ojibwes, Ottawas, and Potawatomis announced that they would leave the next day. They agreed, however, to participate before leaving in a night assault on the fort. At midnight, Indians carrying torches began again to invade the clearing around Fort Recovery. The torches, however, attracted hailstorms of American fire. The Indians' night attack, Alder recalled, just "got a great many killed and wounded." The following morning the Ojibwes, Ottawas, and Potawatomis left. Buckongahelas and his 400 reinforcements would arrive soon, but the Indians, who had failed to capture even the blockhouse on the Wabash, had lost their willingness to continue the campaign. Abandoning their siege, they began moving back to the Glaize.

The American losses were substantial: McMahon and Hartshorne were dead; Taylor and Drake were wounded. In all, the Americans had lost 23 killed, 29 wounded, and three captured. The Indians, however, had suffered far worse. Their casualties, Wells estimated, were 50 killed and 100 wounded. There also had been British losses and, as the Indians retreated toward the Glaize, the prominent Detroit trader Jean-Baptiste Beaubien died of his wounds.

When news of the battle reached Fort Miamis, Maj. William Campbell sent dispatches to Detroit and Newark asking for reinforcements. Simcoe, who promised to provide them, wrote on July 10, "I conceive war inevitable." When Little Turtle and other chiefs sought a firm commitment that British regulars would fight with the Indians, Simcoe promised that they would. In August, he said, he would arrive at Fort Miamis, assume command of an army of British soldiers and Upper Canadian militiamen, and address the Indians at a war council.

At Fort Greeneville, Wayne was almost ready to advance to the Maumee. The men who had joined Clark's French Revolutionary Legion had dispersed. Fort Massac guarded the river from any Spanish advance. He also had received specific orders on Fort Miamis: if Wayne concluded that an attack on the fort was certain to succeed and was necessary to defeat the Ohio Indians, he was authorized to proceed with such an operation. Wayne had managed to assemble for his campaign almost 2,000 US Army officers and soldiers. Many, however, doubted that such a small force would escape the fate of St. Clair's army. On July 14, Capt. Daniel Bradley wrote in his journal "There is orders for two thousand militia from Kentucky to join. If they do, or near it, I think we shall go safe but if they do not and we move I fear the consequences." Scott had promised to arrive at Fort Washington by July 20. There the officers wagered on whether he would bring with him even 1,000 men. Washington's suppression of Clark's expedition had angered many in Kentucky. War with the Chickamauga Cherokee, moreover, had diverted a portion of the Kentucky militia to the Southwest Territory.

Many Kentuckians, however, saw in Wayne's campaign an opportunity that might never recur. On March 31, 1788, the famous frontiersman Brand Ballard had returned to his home near what is now Shelbyville, Kentucky, to find 20 Delaware attacking Ballard's Station. His rifle balls had killed six. The raiders, however, had fled with the scalps of five of the six members of Ballard's family. Now men like Ballard came forward to fight a final battle that would end Indian raiding forever. On July 17, ferryboats from the new settlement at Newport began to cross the Ohio to Cincinnati. First they carried Brig. Gen. Robert Todd's three-battalion Northern Kentucky Brigade, and then Brig. Gen. Thomas Barbee's three-battalion Southern Kentucky Brigade. Almost 1,700 Kentucky horsemen had volunteered and the men he'd brought, Scott boasted, were "all damned fighting fellows." On July 25, Scott reached Fort Greeneville with Todd's brigade. Barbee's brigade, left behind to escort a large food convoy, would join the army as it marched. On July 27, Wayne sent a last letter to Knox: "The legion will advance at 6 o'clock tomorrow morning … Our advance will be as rapid and secret as the nature of the case will admit … We have had and shall have a many-headed monster to contend with and yet I have the most flattering hopes of triumphing over all our enemies both in front and rear."

FROM FORT RECOVERY TO FALLEN TIMBERS

Wayne's Trace led northwest to Fort Recovery, toward Kekionga at the head of the Maumee. Hartshorne's Road led northeast to Girty's Town, toward the Glaize and Fort Miamis. Which Wayne chose would disclose to enemy scouts their first clue to the army's destination.

This monument marks the site of Wayne's ninth camp, known as Camp Stillwater.
(Photograph by Robert Hart)

After leaving Maj. John Buell and about 520 men at Fort Greeneville, the Americans marched northwest. On July 28, they reached the army's ninth camp. On July 29, they halted at the army's tenth camp, a mile west of Fort Recovery. That evening, Wayne assembled those who had fought at the fort a month before. He grabbed their shoulders and shook their hands, remembered Joseph Fitzgerald, a private in Gibson's rifle company, and called them "the bravest boys in the world." On July 30, Wayne left the recovering Lt. Samuel Drake and 40 men at Fort Recovery. After adding Gibson's and Bissell's companies to his army, he continued his deception. Instead of continuing northwest toward Kekionga, he marched northeast to the army's 11th camp.

On July 31, soldiers labored for ten hours to build a 100yds-long bridge over an area of swamp. At the same time a party of soldiers began cutting a road north to the St. Marys River. They followed a line laid out by Robert Newman and Daniel Cooper, Kentucky surveyors who had arrived at Fort Greeneville with Scott's horsemen. On August 1, the army advanced to the St. Marys. At its 12th camp, the army paused to await the arrival of Barbee's brigade and its food convoy. There Wayne began building a fort to guard the army's supply road. The tiny fortification, named for Vice-President John Adams, would have two 18ft-square blockhouses, joined by 24ft-long picket walls at right angles. Newman and Cooper were told to begin marking the army's next line of advance toward the Glaize. On the morning of August 2, however, Newman could not be found. The prior evening, he had gone beyond the army's pickets. O'Hara, he'd said, had told him to look at the line of advance. But O'Hara had given no such orders. Newman, Wayne feared, had left to warn the Indians that the American army was advancing toward the Glaize.

On August 3, Wayne's fear of treachery deepened. At about 3.00pm a beech tree fell on the tents of Wayne and his aide Capt. Henry De Butts. Both escaped death by inches. An investigation then revealed why the tree had fallen. One side had been burned away. As rumors spread that the American commander had been killed, work on Fort Adams stopped. Unable to stand unaided, the severely bruised Wayne had himself placed on his horse. Riding through the camp, he shouted that the army would go forward as soon as Barbee's Brigade arrived with the supply convoy. A few hours later, the Kentuckians and their food reached the camp. At 5.00am on August 4 the Americans renewed their advance. They left an unhappy Lt. James Underhill and 70 mostly ill men to finish and garrison Fort Adams. Underhill had good

The Glaize today, with the Auglaize River to the left and the Maumee to the right. The name is derived from the French *au glaize*, the place with clay soil. (Photograph by John Stanton)

reason for worry. That day, 18 Delaware attacked four men working near Fort Recovery. After pausing at their 13th and 14th camps, the Americans moved toward the Auglaize River. On August 6, they reached their 15th camp. Scouts reported that Gray Eyes Town, a Delaware village, was only a few miles ahead. Kentucky horsemen sent forward to attack it found the village recently deserted.

The Americans then moved down the Auglaize. On August 7, they halted at the army's 16th camp. On August 8, they marched through thousands of acres of cornfields. After passing deserted Buckongahelas's and Big Cat's Town on the left bank, and Capt. Johnny's Town on the right, they reached the Glaize at last. There, across the Maumee from Blue Jacket's Town and downstream from nearby Little Turtle's Town, they built their 17th camp. Newman's warning had barely reached the Indians at the Glaize in time. Joseph Kelly, a ten-year-old Delaware captive, remembered their panicked flight. The Indians, he recalled, "had no time to take any provisions, and only a few kettles and blankets, but hurrying into their canoes pushed off down the Maumee." John Brickell, a 13-year-old adopted Delaware, had returned from a hunting trip to find the villages empty. "Next morning," Brickell recalled, "an Indian runner came down the river and gave the alarm whoop ... The Indians told us white men were upon us and we must run for our lives. We scattered like a flock of partridges, leaving our breakfast cooking on the fire. The Kentucky riflemen saw our smoke and came to it, and just missed me as I passed them in my flight through the corn."

As the Americans began building the first of their permanent forts on the Maumee, the Indians prepared for the battle to come. Forty-seven miles down the river, 200 Shawnee, 300 Delaware, and 100 Miami warriors gathered at the foot of the Maumee Rapids. Hundreds of Ottawa and Wyandot warriors joined them. About 400 Iroquois, uncertain whether they would join in a battle against the Americans, arrived as well. Indian messengers were racing to seek reinforcements. Alder was riding to Sandusky to summon still more Wyandots. Joseph Brant and about 100 Mohawks were expected shortly. In response to Campbell's urgent request, the British dispatched all the reinforcements that could be gathered to Fort Miamis. England detached from the Detroit garrison two more companies of the 24th, and 20 artillerymen. Royal Navy Capt. Alexander Harrow, commander of the British ships on Lake Erie, sent two guns. Bunbury assembled 140 men from the Queen's Rangers, the permanent territorial military force of Upper Canada. Colonel François Bâby, the commander of the Detroit area militia,

In 1827, Mary Wells Wolcott (Ahmaquahzahquah), a daughter of William Wells and granddaughter of Little Turtle, began building this house. It is now a museum in Maumee, Ohio, with Wells family memorabilia. (Courtesy of the Maumee Valley Historical Society)

sent his brother Capt. James Bâby and 100 militiamen. Matthew Elliot's business partner Capt. William Caldwell, whose rangers had fought the Americans in Ohio during the Revolutionary War, quickly recruited two "Volunteer Companies of Refugees."

On August 11, as the British schooner *Chippewa*, and cutters *Brazen* and *Spitfire*, arrived at Fort Miamis with the reinforcements, Wayne made a last attempt to avoid marching down the Maumee. His army had only a limited supply of food. An encounter with the British at Fort Miamis, moreover, would dramatically increase the chances of the war Jay was trying to avoid. The Indians' debacle at Fort Recovery, he thought, might have left them willing to negotiate a peace. He sent Wells, McClellan, the adopted Shawnee Christopher Miller, and three other scouts down the Maumee on a dangerous mission. They were to return with prisoners who could disclose whether the Indians still were determined to fight.

This painting by Hermann Wiebe depicts Fort Defiance. (Courtesy of Weaner, Zimmerman, Bacon, Yoder, and Hubbard Ltd., Defiance, Ohio)

On August 12, Wayne learned that Newman had not been the only spy in his army. Kentucky Capt. Richard Taylor, whose ten-year-old son Zachary would become the 12th US president, found a letter left beyond the Americans' camp for Indians to find. Wayne ordered its author, Newman's fellow surveyor Daniel Cooper, arrested. On the same day, Wells, with a shattered wrist, McClellan, with a wounded shoulder, and the other scouts returned with two prisoners. The Indians, the prisoners said, were talking of making peace with the Americans unless the British fought with them. On August 13, Wayne sent Miller to the Indians with a message. If the Indians wanted peace, they should meet the Americans at a peace council between the Glaize and Roche de Bout, an Ottawa village 40 miles down the Maumee. On the same day, the Americans completed their fort on the Maumee. Its four blockhouses, connected by four 60ft-long walls with 12ft-high pickets, impressed Scott. "I defy the English, the Indians, and all the devils of Hell to take it," he said. Wayne then named the stronghold Fort Defiance.

As a downpour delayed Wayne's planned advance on August 14, the Indian commanders convened at a camp a mile from the foot of the Maumee Rapids. Little Turtle, who doubted that the British would fight the Americans, argued for peace. The other war chiefs, however, were eager for battle. Their losses at Fort Recovery had not dispelled the Indians' contempt for the enemy they had defeated so easily at Wabash. Wayne's soldiers, they believed, could defend a fort, but would not be a formidable foe on a battlefield. "The Indians," remembered Alder, "talked as though it would be an easy victory." The Indian women and children went 9 miles down the Maumee to a camp at the mouth of Swan Creek. Except for a few Mohawks, the 400 Iroquois joined them. The Indian commanders then chose as a battlefield ground where a tornado had left a thicket of fallen trees. A mile southwest of the Indian camp, it would be remembered as Fallen Timbers. Little Turtle's doubts about British support, however, were not ignored. Pressed for proof that the British would fight, Alexander McKee arranged a satisfactory compromise. Caldwell's companies, led by Capts. Daniel McKillip and Thomas Smith, would fight dressed as Indians. Campbell's 42nd Regiment companies, the British artillerymen, Bunbury's Queen's Rangers, and Bâby's Canadian militiamen would all remain at Fort Miamis. If the Indians failed to defeat the Americans, the men and guns at the fort could protect their retreat.

When Miller reached the Indian camp, he was sent back to Wayne with an offer. If the Americans would remain at the Glaize for ten days, he was told, Indian representatives would arrive to talk about peace. The offer, Alexander McKee wrote to Simcoe, "is entirely calculated to gain a few days time in hopes that the Potawatomis and Indians about Detroit may increase their strength."

On August 15, Wayne left Maj. Thomas Hunt and a garrison of 100 men at Fort Defiance. As the Chickasaws and Choctaws returned home, Maj. William Price and a battalion of 150 Kentucky horsemen led the army forward. The Americans advanced to their 18th camp near Snake's Town, an empty Shawnee village. There Miller returned with the Indian offer. Wayne's response was to continue to advance. On August 16, his army went forward to its 19th camp. There a courier arrived with alarming news from Lt. Col. Thomas Butler, the commandant of Fort Fayette. On July 16, he reported, 37 men opposed to the whiskey tax had attacked Brig. Gen. John Neville's house, Bower Hill. The defenders had killed one and wounded six.

Butler then had sent a sergeant and 12 soldiers to guard the house. On July 17, about 700 men had overwhelmed them, killing one and wounding two US Army soldiers before burning Neville's house to the ground.

The news did not distract the American commander from his mission. On August 17, after placing the army on half rations, Wayne led his army further down the Maumee to its 20th camp. On August 18, the Americans reached Roche de Bout. At the abandoned Ottawa village, named for a large rock in the Maumee, they built their 21st camp. When scouts reported that the Americans had reached Roche de Bout, the Indian warriors began assuming their positions at Fallen Timbers. The next day, they believed, there would be a battle. The Canadians were certain that the Indians would prevail. "I am as confident as ever," wrote a Canadian militia officer, "that they will conquer their enemy."

On August 19, however, the Americans did not advance. The cautious Wayne instead wanted more information. From the Americans' 21st camp an Indian trail led north along the Maumee to Fort Miamis. Wayne ordered Price's horsemen to go forward to search for Indians. About 5 miles up the trail, the Kentuckians reached the area of fallen trees, detected Indians, and retired. That, Price told Wayne, was where the Indians would fight. The civilians, wagons, and oxen, Wayne decided, would remain at the 21st camp. At what would be remembered as Fort Deposit, a 2ft-deep ditch and logs piled on a 2ft-high embankment would protect them. Captain Zebulon Pike, a Wabash survivor, and 200 men would stay as their guard. The rest of the army, Wayne announced, would go forward at 5.00am. After two-and-a-half years, his soldiers were at last within striking distance of an Indian army that was waiting for battle. "This," remembered Wayne's aide Lt. William Henry Harrison, "was all that was wanted by the American commander."

The photograph, taken at a time of low water on the Maumee River, shows Roche de Bout today. (Photograph by John Stanton)

The lower Maumee River

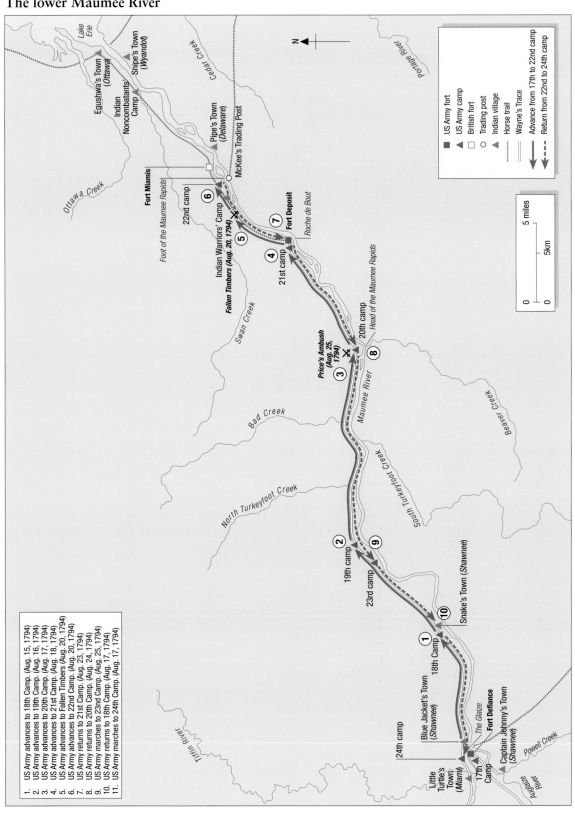

Legend:
- ■ US Army fort
- ▲ US Army camp
- □ British fort
- ○ Trading post
- ▲ Indian village
- ‖ Horse trail
- ⋯ Wayne's Trace
- → Advance from 17th to 22nd camp
- ⇢ Return from 22nd to 24th camp

0 — 5 miles
0 — 5km

1. US Army advances to 18th Camp. (Aug. 15, 1794)
2. US Army advances to 19th Camp. (Aug. 16, 1794)
3. US Army advances to 20th Camp. (Aug. 17, 1794)
4. US Army advances to 21st Camp. (Aug. 18, 1794)
5. US Army advances to Fallen Timbers (Aug. 20, 1794)
6. US Army advances to 22nd Camp. (Aug. 20, 1794)
7. US Army returns to 21st Camp. (Aug. 23, 1794)
8. US Army returns to 20th Camp. (Aug. 24, 1794)
9. US Army marches to 23rd Camp. (Aug. 25, 1794)
10. US Army returns to 18th Camp. (Aug. 17, 1794)
11. US Army marches to 24th Camp. (Aug. 17, 1794)

Lake Erie
Snipe's Town (*Wyandot*)
Egushwa's Town (*Ottawa*)
Indian Noncombatants' Camp
Cedar Creek
Portage River
Pipe's Town (*Delaware*)
McKee's Trading Post
Fort Miamis
Ottawa Creek
Foot of the Maumee Rapids
22nd camp
Indian Warriors' Camp
Fallen Timbers (Aug. 20, 1794)
6
5
4
7
Fort Deposit
Roche de Bout
21st camp
Swan Creek
20th camp
Head of the Maumee Rapids
Price's Ambush (Aug. 25, 1794)
3
8
Maumee River
Bad Creek
Beaver Creek
South Turkeyfoot Creek
North Turkeyfoot Creek
2
9
19th camp
23rd camp
Snake's Town (*Shawnee*)
10
18th Camp
1
Blue Jacket's Town (*Shawnee*)
The Glaize
Fort Defiance
Captain Johnny's Town (*Shawnee*)
Powell Creek
24th camp
Tiffin River
Little Turtle's Town (*Miami*)
17th Camp
Auglaize River

THE BATTLE OF FALLEN TIMBERS

On August 20 the Americans awoke in a heavy downpour. When the rain stopped at about 7.15am, Wayne ordered his drummers to beat "Assembly," the signal for his units to take their places in the columns of march. The army's drums, however, had been left exposed to the unexpected rain. Wayne previously had selected a group of officers who would carry his orders to unit commanders during the battle. Now they raced to tell his officers to assemble their men.

By 7.30am the Americans were moving forward from Fort Deposit. As Pike watched with his 15-year-old son Zebulon, who would become a famous explorer, Capt. William Kibbey's 65 scouts crossed the Maumee to their position as guards of the army's far right flank. Price's 150 horsemen, divided into seven units about 100yds apart, then rode forward on a front more than 1,000yds wide; 100yds ahead of each of Price's units, two men rode as the army's lead scouts. About 400yds behind the Kentuckians, Capt. John Cooke led the army's Advance Infantry Guard, two columns of 37 men detached from companies of the 3rd and 4th Sublegions. One hundred yards to their rear Capt. Robert Miscampbell rode with a squad of his Black Horse Troop. 150yds behind the dragoons came Capt. Howell Lewis's Advance Irregular Guard, which consisted of his light infantry company flanked by platoons of Capt. Daniel Tilton's rifle company. 150yds behind Lewis's irregulars, rode the other three squads of Miscampbell's dragoon troop. One hundred yards back on the Indian trail, Wayne rode at the head of the army's artillery column. With him were the officers who would carry his orders in battle: Maj. John Mills, Capts. Henry De Butts, Thomas Lewis, and Harrison. Next came the lead artillery companies, led by Lt. Percy Pope and Capt. Mahlon Ford; a train of horses carrying the army's 16 howitzers and munitions; and the rear artillery companies, commanded by Capt. Moses Porter and Lt. Ebenezer Massey. Behind them, rear guard units paralleled those ahead of the artillery column. Lieutenant Leonard Covington's Bay Horse Troop provided the dragoons, Capt. Daniel Bradley's company the light infantrymen, and Capt. William Preston's company the riflemen. Then came Capt. John Reed's rear guard of 1st and 2nd Sublegion infantrymen.

About 150yds to the right of the trail, Wilkinson led a column of about 340 regular infantrymen, which moved forward in four files. First came the 220 infantrymen of Capt. Jacob Kingsbury's 3rd Sublegion. Its 2nd Battalion, led by Capt. William Lewis, preceded its 1st Battalion, commanded by Capt. John Heth. Behind them marched the 120 men of Capt. William Peters's 1st Sublegion. Its 2nd Battalion, led by Capt. Hamilton Armstrong, advanced ahead of its 1st Battalion, commanded by Capt. Daniel Britt.

This map of the battlefield, probably drawn by an American officer, appeared in *New York Magazine* in 1794. (Collection of the New York Historical Society. Negative 858100)

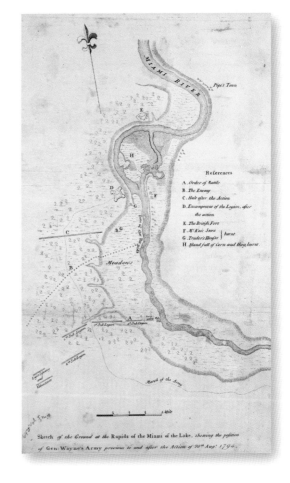

For decades after the battle, Ottawas left offerings at Turkeyfoot Rock, now at Fallen Timbers State Memorial in Maumee, Ohio. Before the battle, they told early settlers, a spirit appeared on the boulder in the guise of a wild turkey, warning the Ottawas not to fight. Others associated the rock with the Ottawa chief Turkey Foot (Masasa), who fell at Fallen Timbers. (Author's photograph)

About 100yds to the right of Wilkinson's column rode three squads of Lt. John Webb's Gray Horse Troop. 150yds beyond them marched the light infantrymen of Kingsbury's company, led by Lt. Bernard Gaines. 150yds to their right, Webb rode forward with his troop's other squad. 100yds beyond them, Capt. Uriah Springer led forward the 110 men in his 3rd Sublegion Rifle Battalion. First the riflemen in his company, and then those in Capt. Richard Sparks's, advanced in single file, 2yds apart.

About 150yds to the left of the Indian trail, Lt. Col. John Hamtramck led a column paralleling Wilkinson's. First came the 220 infantrymen of Maj. Jonathan Haskell's 4th Sublegion. Captain John Cooke's 2nd Battalion, led by Capt. Benjamin Price, moved ahead of its 1st Battalion, led by Capt. Jacob Slough. Then came the 120 men of Lt. Col. David Strong's 2nd Sublegion. Its 2nd Battalion, led by Capt. Samuel Andrews, preceded its 1st Battalion, led by Capt. Edward Miller. To the left of Hamtramck's column, advancing flank units paralleled those on Wilkinson's right. Capt. Solomon Van Rensselaer's Sorrell Horse Troop provided the dragoons and Capt. Joseph Brock's company the light infantrymen. Beyond them were the 110 men in Capt. Alexander Gibson's 4th Sublegion Rifle Battalion. First came his company, veterans of Fort Recovery, and then Capt. Edward Butler's. The rest of Scott's Kentucky horsemen guarded the army's far left flank and rear. Four hundred yards to the left of Gibson's riflemen, Todd's Northern Kentucky Brigade advanced in long columns. Four hundred yards behind Reed's infantrymen, Brig. Gen. Thomas Barbee's three-battalion Southern Kentucky Brigade rode forward in long lines.

At the head of the advancing Americans, Price's Kentuckians walked their horses forward through terrain that they had explored the day before. Those on the right rode through the 6ft-high prairie grass of a 600–900yds-wide floodplain, through which the 300yds-wide Maumee River flowed. To the left of the floodplain, above the tall grass and brilliant August prairie flowers, rose a 35yds-high ridge, which steep ravines punctuated at intervals. For the first 200–300yds to the left of the ridge's edge the ground was relatively open, covered by large oaks. Further to the left, the woods became a dense thicket of trees, bushes, and brambles.

As Price's horsemen went forward, they looked for two memorable features of the landscape. The first, about 3 miles beyond Roche de Bout, was a mile-long area of high ground in the floodplain known as Presque Isle. The second, about a mile beyond Presque Isle, was the area of fallen trees where they had seen Indians the day before. When the downpour had awakened the waiting Indians, many had concluded that there again would be no battle. As hours passed, about a quarter of the warriors had left their positions and returned to the Indian camp to eat. Now, dispersed six deep in a line about 700yds long, roughly 1,100 Indians and Canadians remained.

On the far Indian left, about 25 Ojibwe waited on the ridge above the Maumee River. To their right there were about 225 Ottawa, led by Egushwa and Little Otter, and about 25 Potawatomi, led by Le Petit Bled. In the center of the Indian line about 200 Shawnee, led by Blue Jacket, Black Hoof, and Black Fish, remained. To their right, there were about 200 Delaware, led by

Buckongahelas, Capt. Pipe, and Big Cat, and then 100 Miami, led by Little Turtle. To their right, there were about 25 Mingos and Mohawks, then about 250 Wyandots led by Tarhe, and, at the extreme right of the Indian line, Caldwell's 70 Canadians in McKillip's and Smith's companies.

As the humid day grew hotter, about 3,300 Americans advanced along a front more than a mile wide, in a parade more than a mile and a half long. The width of the advance divided the dragoons, light infantrymen, and riflemen on the right, who were marching through the floodplain, from the rest of the army, advancing on the ridge. The horsemen and irregulars, some of the officers feared, were too dispersed. Wayne's orders of march and battle addressed how the army's units were to deploy in response to an attack from any direction. The orders, Wilkinson protested, were so "pompous and prolix" that the scattered American units could never be concentrated to fight the Indians effectively. Others doubted whether the army's regular infantry units would be able to form coherent battle lines. Wilkinson's and Hamtramck's infantrymen, marching in columns 300yds apart, were to fight in two lines. The army's operations manual, Steuben's *Regulations*, prescribed that the battalions in such lines each should occupy about 120yds and be separated by about 30yds. If the Indians attacked from ahead of the army, the four 3rd and 4th Sublegion battalions were to form the front line from the point where the artillery ceased to advance. The columns' lead battalions, the 2nd Battalions of the 3rd and 4th Sublegions, were to wheel toward the trail to form the line. The 1st Battalions were to extend it on their flanks, The trailing four battalions of the 1st and 2nd Sublegions were then to form the second line about 200yds to the rear.

The terrain, however, would make it hard for the sublegion commanders to form coherent lines. The 3rd and 1st Sublegion column was marching forward across steep ravines. The 4th and 2nd Sublegion column, Wilkinson remembered, was advancing through "an impervious thicket." There, remembered Scott's aide de camp Francis Jones, "it was difficult to see a man at 10 yards." As the heads of the American columns diverged and the men on the left kept falling behind, Wayne halted the army at intervals so that his commanders could practice forming battle lines. After about two hours, Price's Kentuckians stopped a half mile ahead of the area where they had seen Indians the day before. Some took last drinks of water, others took off their sweat-soaked shirts. Then the two men ahead of each unit went forward again. Walking their horses slowly around fallen trunks and branches, the rest of the Kentuckians followed 100yds behind.

LEFT
The appearance today of the ridge upon which the army was advancing at the time of the attack, as seen from the position of Springer's Rifle Battalion. (Author's photograph)

RIGHT
The appearance today of the area where Wayne halted the artillery column's advance on the Indian trail, looking northeast. (Author's photograph)

THE AMERICAN RIGHT, AUGUST 20, 1794, 10.00AM (pp. 64–65)

In the 6ft-high grass of the Maumee River floodplain, on the American right flank, 100 Ottawa and Ojibwe Indians have driven 50 American light infantrymen back about 200yds. Now, reinforced by riflemen, the light infantrymen have stopped the Indian advance. An Ottawa Indian (1) who has crept forward through the grass is attacking the Americans. An American light infantryman (2) is using his "improved musket" to fire a load of shot into the grass. He wears the uniform of an American infantryman, a blue, white-lined, short coat with red facings and white buttons, white vest and trousers, and a black, cocked hat with bearskin crest, leather cockade, and colored plume. The color of the hat trim and plumes identified soldiers' sublegions (1st: white, 2nd: red, 3rd: yellow, 4th: green). This soldier's white hat trim and plume identify his unit as Lt. Bernard Gaines's 1st Sublegion Light Infantry Co. A light infantryman (3) is reloading his weapon as another (4) lies dead. Another American soldier (5) has locked into place a folding spear. His blue jacket with red shoulder wings, bounded at the waist by a red band, mark him as a rifleman. His yellow hat trim and plume identify his unit as Capt. Uriah Springer's 3rd Sublegion Rifle Battalion. As another rifleman (6) locks his folding spear, Springer (7), waving an espontoon, is shouting to his riflemen to hurry forward. In the distance, puffs of smoke rising from the grass (8) show where Indians have fired their muskets.

When Lt. William Sudduth had asked for men to ride ahead of his unit, Thomas Moore and William Steele had volunteered for the dangerous duty. At about 9.45am, they reached the Ottawas and Potawatomis in the Indian line. The first fire of the battle killed them both. Sudduth's horsemen then went forward to within 20yds of the Indians. Musket fire hit them, he recalled, "with a tremendous roar at a very short distance." The Kentuckians fell back about 40yds. Ottawas and Potawatomis rushed forward, but fire from Kentucky rifles halted them. Soon, however, Shawnees in overwhelming numbers appeared on the Kentuckians' left. When a ball struck his horse, Sudduth recalled, "I gave him the spur and pushed him on, the blood gushing out of the wound. He ran about one hundred and fifty yards and stopped. I leaped off." The Kentuckians fled 70yds ahead of pursuing Indians. Those on the right rode down into the floodplain. Those near the Indian trail raced back toward the next line of Americans, Cooke's Advance Infantry Guard. Hearing the fire ahead, 37 infantrymen, led by Cooke, had formed a line to the right of the Indian trail. Another 37, led by Lt. John Steele, had formed a line to their left. Cooke remembered his orders to fire on any soldiers retreating without orders. When the Kentuckians came within 80yds of his men, a volley of musket balls awaited them. The startled horsemen then raced around the infantrymen toward the main body of the army.

The Indians soon reached Cooke's infantrymen. His men, Cooke remembered, fired a volley "in very good order." But when Indians began outflanking them to the right, they "got into confusion and began to fly." Cooke and about a dozen of his men then joined Steele's line. Within a few minutes the commanders in the main body of the American army learned that a battle had begun. When Wilkinson saw horsemen riding back through the tall grass in the floodplain, he ordered his infantry column to halt. When about 50 Kentuckians reached Hamtramck's and Wayne's columns, they reported that hundreds of Indians were coming.

"Prepare," the American commander shouted, "to receive the enemy in front in two lines." Wayne's staff officers sped away to confirm that his units were moving to the proper positions to oppose an Indian attack from the front. Howell Lewis was to form his light infantrymen ahead of the army. Tilton's riflemen were to disperse behind them. Gaines was to lead his light infantry company forward to a position on Lewis's right. Brock's company was to advance to Lewis's left. Behind them, Wilkinson and Hamtramck were to form their infantry lines. In the rear, Barbee's horsemen were to ride to the American far left flank, to a position behind Todd's Kentuckians.

As the sublegion and regular infantry battalion commanders began marking the course of their lines through the woods, Cooke's 50 remaining men tried to hold the Ottawas and Potawatomis back. They stood their ground, Cooke remembered, long enough to deliver three volleys. Then, he recalled, "we were obliged to retreat and fire for about one hundred yards, by which time they came on so close and in such numbers that I was obliged to direct the guards to make the best of their way to their respective companies." Cooke's fleeing men soon reached Howell Lewis' light infantrymen, who were forming the next American defensive line. As the regular infantrymen ran through Lewis's left platoon, many of his light infantrymen joined them. After pursuing his men for 40yds, Lewis brought them back into line with the right platoon. The Ottawas and Potawatomis then appeared about 100yds ahead of the light infantrymen and opened a heavy fire.

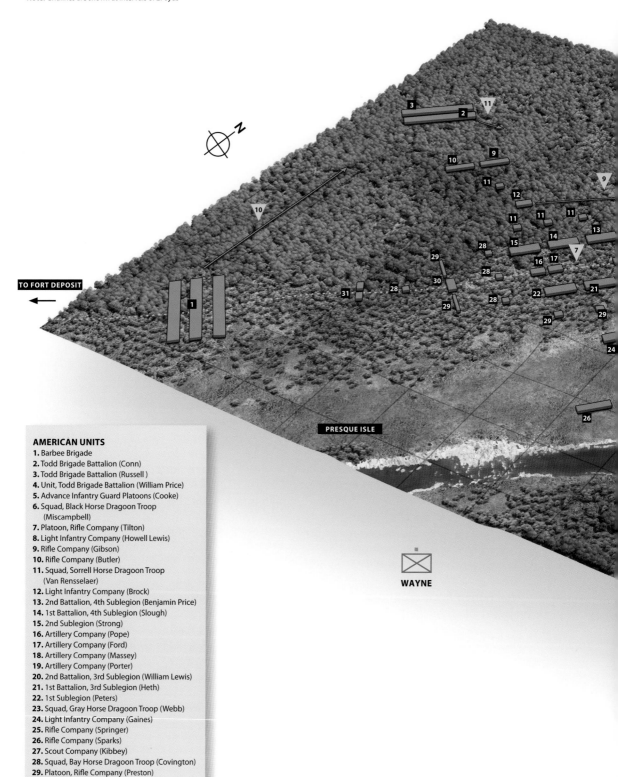

Note: Gridlines are shown at intervals of 270yds

TO FORT DEPOSIT

PRESQUE ISLE

WAYNE

AMERICAN UNITS
1. Barbee Brigade
2. Todd Brigade Battalion (Conn)
3. Todd Brigade Battalion (Russell)
4. Unit, Todd Brigade Battalion (William Price)
5. Advance Infantry Guard Platoons (Cooke)
6. Squad, Black Horse Dragoon Troop
   (Miscampbell)
7. Platoon, Rifle Company (Tilton)
8. Light Infantry Company (Howell Lewis)
9. Rifle Company (Gibson)
10. Rifle Company (Butler)
11. Squad, Sorrell Horse Dragoon Troop
    (Van Rensselaer)
12. Light Infantry Company (Brock)
13. 2nd Battalion, 4th Sublegion (Benjamin Price)
14. 1st Battalion, 4th Sublegion (Slough)
15. 2nd Sublegion (Strong)
16. Artillery Company (Pope)
17. Artillery Company (Ford)
18. Artillery Company (Massey)
19. Artillery Company (Porter)
20. 2nd Battalion, 3rd Sublegion (William Lewis)
21. 1st Battalion, 3rd Sublegion (Heth)
22. 1st Sublegion (Peters)
23. Squad, Gray Horse Dragoon Troop (Webb)
24. Light Infantry Company (Gaines)
25. Rifle Company (Springer)
26. Rifle Company (Sparks)
27. Scout Company (Kibbey)
28. Squad, Bay Horse Dragoon Troop (Covington)
29. Platoon, Rifle Company (Preston)
30. Light Infantry Company (Bradley)
31. Rear Infantry Guard Platoons (Reed)

INDIAN UNITS
A. Right Wing (Canadian Volunteer Companies, Wyandots, Mingos, and Mohawks)
B. Center (Miami, Delaware, Shawnee)
C. Left Wing (Potawatomi, Ottawa, Ojibwe)

BLUE JACKET

TO INDIAN WARRIORS' CAMP

INDIAN TRAIL

MAUMEE RIVER

EVENTS

1. Ottawa attack Sudduth's unit of Price's battalion.

2. Scattered units of Price's battalion retreat to advancing American columns.

3. Ojibwe and Ottawa advance into floodplain, seeking to turn the American right.

4. Ottawa pursuing units of Price's battalion attack Cooke's advance infantry guard.

5. Shawnee, Delaware and Miami advance toward American columns.

6. Canadians and Wyandots advance searching for American left flank.

7. Regular infantry companies begin to form two lines. Artillery companies move to flanks of lines. Dragoon squads assemble in troops behind the artillery companies.

8. Gaines's light infantry company advances to form right of irregular defense line.

9. Brock's light infantry company advances to form left of irregular defense line.

10. Barbee's brigade advances toward rear of Conn's and Russell's battalions.

11. Conn's and Russell's battalions advance on far American left.

THE INDIAN ATTACK

On August 20, 1794, the Indian army attacks the marching American army at approximately 9.45 to 10.00am

As the shotguns of Lewis's men responded, Kingsbury's 3rd Sublegion battalions began forming their portion of the front infantry line. Captain William Lewis's 2nd Battalion wheeled to occupy its left and Capt. John Heth's 1st advanced to form its right. Thirty yards to the left of Lewis's men, Haskell's 4th Sublegion infantrymen extended the line at a 30-degree angle to the rear. There, Cooke's battalion, led by Capt. Benjamin Price, occupied the right and Capt. Jacob Slough's battalion the left. The front-line artillery, dragoon, and rifle company commanders found the ground their units would occupy on the infantrymen's flanks. Pope's artillery company moved toward its assigned posting on the 3rd Sublegion's right and Ford's to its on the 4th Sublegion's left. Miscampbell's dragoon troop was to assemble behind Pope's guns and Springer's rifle companies to form on their right. Van Rensselaer's horsemen were to be behind Ford's guns and Gibson's rifle companies to their left.

About 200yds behind them, the rear-line units occupied their assigned positions. Captain William Peters's 1st Sublegion infantrymen formed behind the 3rd Sublegion, with Capt. Daniel Britt's 2nd Battalion on the right and Capt. Hamilton Armstrong's 1st Battalion on the left. Lieutenant Colonel David Strong's 2nd Sublegion men took their positions behind the 4th Sublegion, with Capt. Samuel Andrews 2nd Battalion on the right and Capt. Edward Miller's 1st Battalion on the left. The rear line battalions, which were smaller than full-strength companies, were able to take their positions quickly. The 2nd Sublegion battalions, Capt. Benjamin Price recalled, formed their line within five minutes. The second line artillerymen and dragoons then moved toward their flanks. Massey's artillerymen were to be on the right and Webb's dragoons to assemble behind them. Porter's guns were to be on the left and Covington's dragoons behind them.

As Miscampbell led his Black Horse Troop back toward its assigned position, he met Wilkinson. What, the Right Wing commander asked, was happening ahead. "Everything," Miscampbell replied, "is confusion."

As the Ottawas and Potawatomis battled Lewis's light infantrymen, the other Indians moved forward. On the Indian left, Ojibwes and Ottawas advanced through the tall grass, hoping to turn the American right flank. On the Indian right, Shawnee, Delaware, Miami, Mohawks, Mingos, Wyandots, and Canadians moved slowly through the thick woods, searching for the Americans' left. The Ojibwes and Ottawas in the floodplain soon reached Gaines's light infantry company. As Wilkinson watched from the ridge, American shotguns blasted into the tall grass. "Firing as warmly as the smallness of their number would permit," he recalled, the light infantrymen tried to hold the Indians back. Alarmed at this assault on the American right, Wilkinson ordered Peters to advance the 1st Sublegion to extend Kingsbury's line. When Pope's howitzers reached their position, they opened fire on the floodplain with shells and then grapeshot. Hailstorms of shell fragments fell on the Ojibwes and Ottawas from above. Swarms of balls cut paths through the tall grass.

Springer's riflemen then advanced to support Gaines's light infantrymen. The Indians, who could find no cover in the grass to protect themselves from the heavy fire, fell back. Wilkinson's aide Lt. Bernard Schaumburgh, sent to determine whether any remained, found one hiding in a clump of bushes. Running to escape Schaumburgh's sword, he died on a light infantryman's bayonet. On the ridge, the Ottawas and Potawatomis continued to push Lewis's light infantrymen and Tilton's scattered riflemen back. Soon the Indians were 150yds ahead of the 3rd Sublegion line. Then, advancing another 70yds, they forced Lewis's and Tilton's men back into Kingsbury's regular infantrymen. But they could advance no further. Turning their guns to the left, Pope's howitzers opened fire with canister shot. Volleys from William Lewis's and Heth's 3rd Sublegion battalions followed. The Ottawa attack, Wilkinson recalled, dwindled into a "desultory fire." Shawnees then arrived to support the Ottawas attacking William Lewis's 3rd Sublegion battalion. As more Shawnees reached the front, they extended the attack to their right, where Cooke had rejoined his 4th Sublegion battalion.

After driving Brock's light infantry company back, the Delaware and Miami arrived to support the Shawnees. The fighting grew fiercer as they extended the attack to Slough's battalion on Cooke's left. Soon Slough fell wounded. At his battalion's far left, nine men in Capt. Maxwell Bines's exposed company fell as the Indians tried to turn the American flank. American reinforcements, however, arrived to relieve the pressure. Gibson's rifle company fought its way through the woods to occupy the ground to Bines's left. Then the guns of Ford's artillery company reached their position. Artillery Sgt. Maj. Thomas Underwood could see Indians in the distance "load and fire, then fall down and load, then rise and fire again." Ford's howitzers targeted them with canister shot. The Shawnee Capt. Tommy remembered the sound of the guns, a loud "waugh! waugh!," and how the woods were full of flying branches, bark, and pieces of metal.

The Indians, Wayne knew, would continue to try to turn the American left. His aides sped with orders for units to advance to extend the American line. The 2nd Sublegion infantry battalions were to go forward to the left of the 4th Sublegion battalions. Todd's 550 horsemen were to dismount, and advance with their rifles to a position beyond the 2nd Sublegion men. Barbee's 800 Kentuckians were to ride in a semicircle far beyond Todd's men, and attack behind the Indians' right flank. When the 2nd Sublegion infantry battalions arrived in front, Capt. Edward Miller's battalion occupied the ground at the far left of the 2nd Sublegion line. As soon as his men reached their position, he remembered, they "immediately received a very heavy fire." Gibson's riflemen moved further left to block the Indians' efforts. Butler's rifle company arrived to join Gibson's. Butler's men, Paxton remembered, had gotten lost in the woods and "had to run or move very rapidly to gain their position in front." Gibson's and Butler's 120 riflemen eliminated the immediate threat to the American left flank. The effort of the Delaware and Miami to turn it was

Note: Gridlines are shown at intervals of 270yds

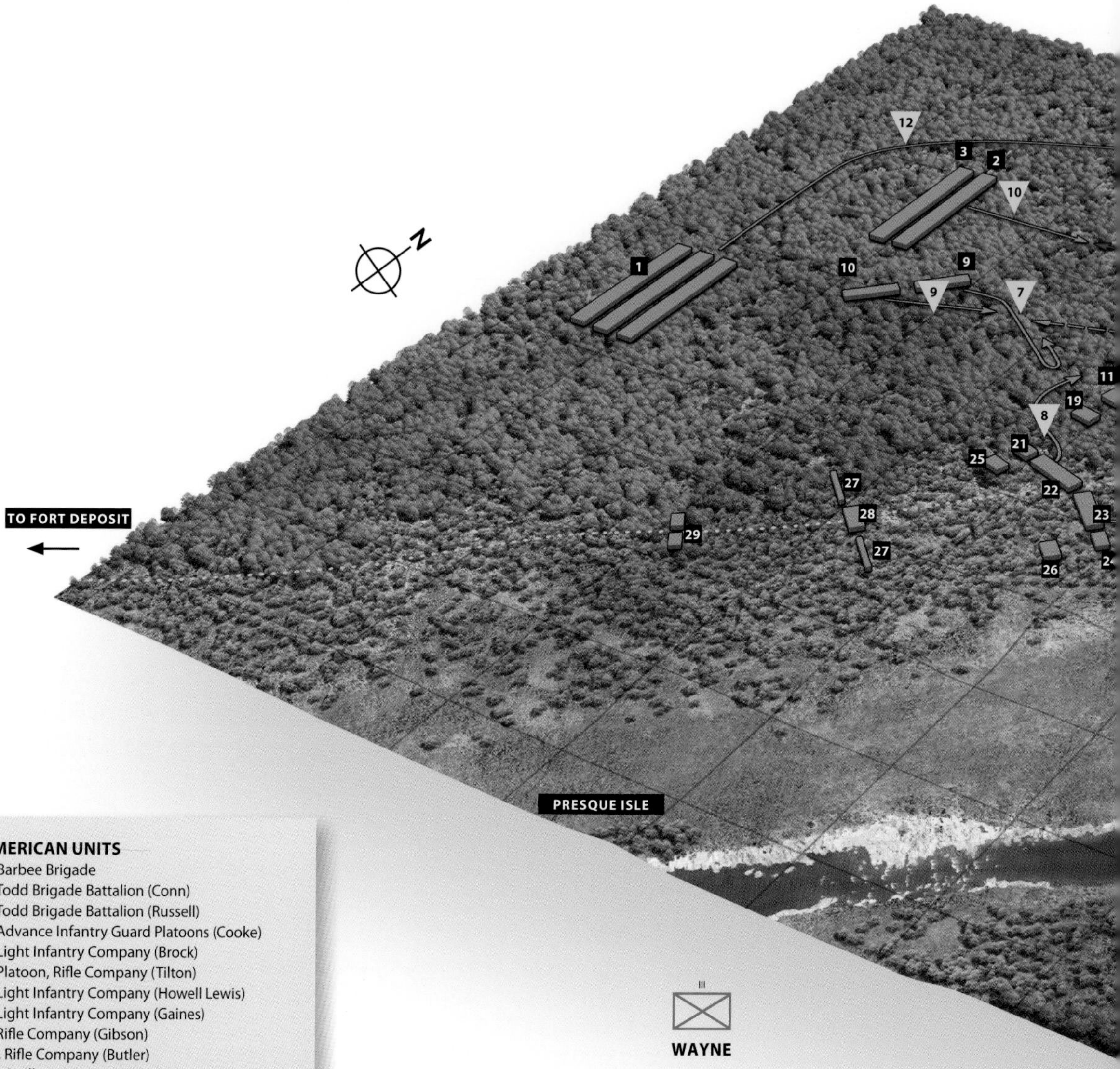

TO FORT DEPOSIT
PRESQUE ISLE
WAYNE

AMERICAN UNITS

1. Barbee Brigade
2. Todd Brigade Battalion (Conn)
3. Todd Brigade Battalion (Russell)
4. Advance Infantry Guard Platoons (Cooke)
5. Light Infantry Company (Brock)
6. Platoon, Rifle Company (Tilton)
7. Light Infantry Company (Howell Lewis)
8. Light Infantry Company (Gaines)
9. Rifle Company (Gibson)
10. Rifle Company (Butler)
11. Artillery Company (Ford)
12. 1st Battalion, 4th Sublegion (Slough)
13. 2nd Battalion, 4th Sublegion (Benjamin Price)
14. 2nd Battalion, 3rd Sublegion (William Lewis)
15. 1st Battalion, 3rd Sublegion (Heth)
16. Artillery Company (Pope)
17. Rifle Company (Springer)
18. Rifle Company (Sparks)
19. Sorrell Horse Dragoon Troop (Van Rensselaer)
20. Black Horse Dragoon Troop (Miscampbell)
21. Artillery Company (Porter)
22. 2nd Sublegion (Strong)
23. 1st Sublegion (Peters)
24. Artillery Company (Massey)
25. Bay Horse Dragoon Troop (Covington)
26. Gray Horse Dragoon Troop (Webb)
27. Platoon, Rifle Company (Preston)
28. Light Infantry Company (Bradley)
29. Rear Infantry Guard Platoons (Reed)
30. Scout Company (Kibbey)

EVENTS

1. Springer's rifle company advances to support Gaines's light infantry company.

2. Ottawas and Ojibwes retreat to ridge.

3. 1st Sublegion extends the right of the American line.

4. Ottawas and Potawatomis force Cooke's advance infantry guard, and then Howell Lewis's irregular advance guard back to near the forming regular infantry line.

5. Advancing Shawnees, Delaware and Miami attack and try to turn left flank of 4th Sublegion line.

6. Brock's light infantry company retreats to American left flank.

7. Gibson's rifle company advances to protect American left flank.

8. 2nd Sublegion extends the left of the American line, and Gibson's rifle company moves left to guard American flank.

9. Butler's rifle company joins Gibson's company.

10. Conn's and Russell's battalions dismount and advance to protect American left flank.

11. Canadian companies and Wyandots reach Conn's and Russell's battalions.

12. Barbee's brigade begins to make wide turn around right of Indian line.

INDIAN UNITS
A. Canadian Volunteer Companies, Wyandots, Mingos, and Mohawks
B. Miami, Delaware, Shawnee
C. Potawatomi and Ottawa
D. Ottawa And Ojibwe

BLUE JACKET

TO INDIAN WARRIORS' CAMP

INDIAN TRAIL

MAUMEE RIVER

THE AMERICAN DEFENSE

Between approximately 10.00 and 10.30am the Americans form a defensive line and repel Indian attempts to turn their flanks.

This coat, worn by Wayne at Fallen Timbers, is displayed at Waynesborough. (Courtesy of Historic Waynesborough)

This 1797 portrait attributed to Robert Field depicts Capt. Solomon Van Rensselaer. (Albany Institute of History and Art, Bequest of Mrs. John Woodworth Gould, 1994.4.4)

exhausted. The Indians' hopes now rested with the 350 Canadians, Wyandots, Mingos, and Mohawks advancing to their right.

Beyond Gibson's and Butler's riflemen, the Canadians and Indians at last reached the far left of the American army. Instead of a few defenders, however, they found there Todd's advancing Kentuckians – the 550 men in Conn's and Russell's battalions. Musket balls flew at Pvt. Garret Burns and his company of Conn's battalion. "We returned the fire," Burns recalled, "rushing on them as they treed to reload. I singled out one Indian and, leveling my rifle, fired. I was behind a tree, as he was, and struck him before he had the same chance as me."

To the Americans at Fallen Timbers, the battle so far had appeared to be chaos in the tall grass and woods. Some American units had fled the attacking Indians. Others had become lost trying to find their places in the battle line. Still others, after reaching their positions, had come under fire from an almost invisible enemy. Beneath the apparent chaos, however, the order anticipated in Wayne's battle plan had emerged. The Indians' attempt to surround the Americans had left them at last fixed in a line. Ahead of them, a parallel American line extended beyond both their flanks. Far to their right, a quarter of Wayne's army was moving forward to attack them from behind.

Around the American commander, Mills, De Butts, Thomas Lewis, and Harrison were constantly departing and arriving. As they left with orders and returned with news, their worries about Wayne's safety grew. Fearing that he would order his soldiers forward and suddenly spur his horse to lead them, they took turns watching, ready to seize his reins. Harrison discreetly articulated the officers' concerns. "General Wayne," the 21-year-old lieutenant finally said, "I am afraid you will go into the fight yourself and forget to give me the necessary field orders." "Perhaps I may," his commander responded, "and if I do, recollect that the standing order for the day is 'Charge the damned rascals with the bayonet.'"

First, however, Wayne would send his horsemen and riflemen against the Indian flanks. On the American right, Springer's riflemen reported that they could find no Indians in the floodplain. Miscampbell went forward with his Black Horse Dragoons to find the Indian left on the ridge. With bugles blowing, his 60 horsemen rode through the gap between William Lewis's and Heth's 3rd Sublegion battalions and turned right and then left to attack the Indians. Sudduth, who had collected about 40 of Price's scattered Kentuckians, rode through a 3rd Sublegion company to join them. Near the edge of the ridge, Sudduth's men found the Indian flank. His Kentuckians, he recalled, "passed their left and wheeled around the extreme point of their left wing."

As Miscampbell's dragoons battled the Indians, their commander fell. More bugles sounded as Webb's horsemen galloped forward to support them. Leaving Sparks's company to protect the army's flank in the floodplain, Springer's riflemen and Gaines's light infantrymen climbed the ridge to join the attack. The Ottawa commanders, Egushwa and Little Otter, both fell with head wounds. Overwhelmed, the Ottawas began retreating.

On the American left, Todd's riflemen were steadily pushing forward. A ball from Burns's rifle killed one of the Wyandots who tried to hold the Kentuckians back. "I saw the Indian fall," Burns remembered, "and rushing on, seized him by the hair. I then put my foot on him to pin him down, and took the scalp off."

Van Rensselaer's Sorrell Horse Dragoons rode forward to join the Kentuckians. Covington's Bay Horse Troop, and Gibson's and Butler's rifle companies followed. A musket ball, an officer recalled, struck Van Rensselaer as he was "in the act of cutting down an Indian." The New York captain, who had celebrated his 20th birthday two weeks before, had "blood rushing from his breast, mouth and nose." He nonetheless, the officer remembered, "refused to be dismounted from his charger, but maintained his seat in the saddle until the enemy were effectually routed." As the American dragoons, riflemen, and light infantrymen assaulted the Indian flanks, their bugles could be heard from both ends of the Indian line. The sounds alarmed the Shawnee, Delaware, and Miami warriors in the center, who feared that they were being surrounded. The "horns," the Delaware Tom Lyons remembered, "way over there go toot, toot; then way over here it go toot, toot; then way over on the other side go toot, toot."

Ahead of Lyons, a line of bayonets extended between the areas where fighting raged on the armies' flanks. Almost 700 American regular infantrymen were in their positions. Behind them, eight young ensigns held the standards of the proud little army's miniature infantry battalions. The infantry officers eagerly awaited Wayne's order to charge. The sublegion commanders had memories to erase. In 1788, Indians had attacked near the mouth of the Wabash a convoy guard led by Peters. At Peters's Defeat, they had killed eight and wounded ten of his 30 men. On January 10, 1791, Kingsbury and 11 soldiers at besieged Dunlap's Station had spent a sleepless night listening to Indians torture to death an American prisoner. On March 27, 1791, Strong had watched Indians massacre 23 of his men at Strong's Defeat near the mouth of the Scioto River. The battalion and company commanders also were impatient. Britt and Price, Slough and Bines, and Capt. Richard Greaton, who led a company in Miller's battalion, had all been wounded at Wabash.

The infantrymen waited with their muskets "trailed," held with one hand so that their bayonets were a head's length in front of their shoulders. At last, pointing their espontoons forward toward the Indians, the officers shouted "Advance. Arms." "I ordered my battalion to charge," remembered Miller, "which was immediately done. The whole line charged nearly at the same time." As Wayne watched, his infantrymen went forward in the "common step." Musket balls felled some, but the others kept moving at a rate of 72 2ft paces a minute. The American commander, one of his officers recalled, "reined up his horse for a dash." When two men seized the reins, he shouted "'Let me go. Damn them. Let me go. Give it to them, Boys.'"

At first, the Indians tried to follow an ordered pattern of retreat. Carrying their dead and wounded, they fell back. In new cover, they would reload and fire. Then they would repeat the pattern, waiting for an opportunity to surround the charging Americans. But the pattern soon lost its order. The relentless advance of Wayne's infantrymen denied the Indians time to pause and reload. The American line, moreover, was too long to surround. Even the young Shawnee chief Tecumseh finally had to abandon his dead brother's body and run.

As Wayne's infantrymen went forward through what had been the center of the Indian line, his horsemen, riflemen, and light infantrymen surged through what had been the Indians' flanks. On the Indian right, the overwhelmed Canadians and Wyandots fought desperately. Soon, however,

THE INDIAN RIGHT, AUGUST 20, 1794, 10.30AM (pp. 76–77)

About 350 Wyandots and Canadian volunteers trying to move around the American left flank have encountered 550 dismounted Kentucky horsemen, and are being driven back through the woods. A Wyandot warrior (1) is running to the Wyandot commander Tarhe (2) to report that American dragoons now are coming in the upper left of the background. Tarhe, wearing an *ofasa*, the traditional kilt of the Wyandots, has been wounded in the left elbow. A Canadian from McKillip's company of volunteers (3), dressed as an Indian, is telling Tarhe that the Canadians to the Wyandots' right are retreating. A Wyandot warrior (4) is firing his musket as another (5) is fleeing the Kentuckians. A Wyandot (6) is asking a wounded friend (7) whether he will need to be carried. Ahead, a Wyandot warrior (8) is reloading his musket as a Kentuckian with a knife (9) races forward to kill him before he can fire again. Behind him, more Kentuckians (10) are coming.

Canadian Capt. Daniel McKillip was dead, and only the wounded Tarhe remained among the senior Wyandot commanders. The Americans, Tom Lyons recalled, "run forward – shoot, shoot; then run among logs and brush. Indians have got to get out and run. Then come Long Knives with pistols and shoot, shoot. Indians run, no stop. Old Tom see too much fight to be trapped. He run into woods. He run like devil. He run till he clear out of danger."

The infantrymen on the American right soon outpaced those advancing on the left. After a few hundred yards, Wilkinson halted the 1st and 3rd Sublegion charge to allow Hamtramck's men to catch up. As Wilkinson's men waited, some of the dragoons on the American left made their way completely through the fleeing Indians. Eighty yards ahead of the 1st and 3rd Sublegion infantrymen, Covington and eight of his Bay Horse Dragoons emerged from the thick woods, rode across their front to the edge of the ridge, and turned left to charge into the retreating Ottawas. Webb's Gray Horse Troop galloped forward to support them. Covington killed two Indians with his saber, and Webb one.

Shawnees falling back from the front passed Delawares arriving late for the battle. Ottawas fleeing from one flank met Wyandots escaping from the other. "The Indians," Alder recalled, "were running both ways, meeting with one another, some breaking right through the horsemen. It became a perfect confusion." There was no refuge in the floodplain, or across the Maumee. American soldiers found the Detroit trader Antoine Laselle, who had fought in Smith's Canadian company, hiding in the tall grass. One of Kibbey's scouts, a black marksman who lived near Columbia, killed three Indians who tried to cross the river. The only path to safety was the trail back to the Indian camp. Barbee's Kentucky battalions, however, now were nearing the end of their long ride around the Indian right. The 800 horsemen were moving slowly through the trees, brush, and fallen logs. But when they reached the trail, the Indians would be trapped.

Alexander McKee, Matthew Elliot, Simon Girty, and some British officers had watched the battle from high ground on the trail. There McKee tried to halt the Indian flight. "McKee," a British officer recalled, "exerted all his powers to make them stand, but in vain. They absolutely refused to fight again."

When Caldwell's Canadians arrived, McKee's party joined the retreat. They had been, Caldwell told McKee, "outgeneraled." The Indians shared that view. Wayne, Tom Lyons said, "be one devil to fight." Outracing

LEFT
After Fallen Timbers, Tecumseh often visited this 1798 cabin, built by the settler James Galloway near the Shawnee chief's boyhood home. At the cabin, now at the Greene County Historical Society in Xenia, Ohio, Galloway's daughter Rebecca taught Tecumseh to read and write. (Author's photograph)

RIGHT
Five years before he became US president, Theodore Roosevelt wrote an account of Fallen Timbers in *Harper's Magazine*. This 1896 engraving by Rufus F. Zogbaum illustrated Roosevelt's "Mad Anthony Wayne's Victory." (Courtesy of *Harper's Magazine*)

THE AMERICAN CENTER, AUGUST 20, 1794, 10.45AM (pp. 80–81)

A line of 4th Sublegion regular infantrymen stretching into the background has begun to advance through the woods against the Indians. The 4th Sublegion commander, Maj. Jonathan Haskell (1) and Lt. William Henry Harrison (2), who has carried to Haskell the order to advance, have dismounted to talk to Capt. Jacob Slough (3), commander of the 1st Battalion of the 4th Sublegion. Wounded at Wabash, Slough has been wounded again. An ensign (4) is carrying the green flag of the 1st Battalion of the 4th Sublegion. A fifer (5), dressed in a musician's uniform of cocked hat, red coat with blue facings, and black vest and trousers, is at the far right of Slough's own 1st Battalion company. To his left, Lt.

William Devin (6), another Wabash survivor, has assumed command of Slough's company. As Devin points his espontoon forward his men are advancing in two ranks, trailing their muskets. One (7) has been hit by an Indian musket ball. Beyond Slough's company, Capt. Maxwell Bines (8) can be seen in the distance. Bines, who was also wounded at Wabash, is leading his 1st Battalion company forward. Ahead, a rifleman (9) from Capt. Daniel Tilton's scattered 3rd Sublegion rifle company has raised his hat to cheer them on.

Barbee's approaching horsemen, the Indians and Canadians narrowly escaped a massacre. They left behind on the field more than 40 bodies. Their casualties, however, were much higher, especially among the Ottawas and Wyandots. "With one or two exceptions," Alder remembered, none of the 20 Wyandot reinforcements he had dispatched from Sandusky survived the battle. But the loss of the Indians could not be measured in dead and wounded. For decades, soldiers in British and American uniforms had marched through the western woods. To the sounds of bagpipes, fifes, and drums, they had advanced to fields like Fallen Timbers. And from such fields, brave Scottish highlanders, resolute English regulars, and American veterans of Saratoga and Yorktown had fled like hunted game. At Fallen Timbers, however, the men running through the woods in terror had for the first time been Indian warriors. The battle, Wayne would report to Knox, had lasted a little more than an hour. The casualties were 40 dead and 90 wounded Legion officers and soldiers, and seven dead and 13 wounded Kentuckians.

Just after 11.00am, the Americans halted at the Indians' camp. They then advanced another mile to the foot of the Maumee Rapids. There, more than 500 miles from Philadelphia, and 200 from the Ohio River, they raised at their twenty-second camp the 15-star flag of the infant United States. And there, as August 20, 1794 reached its end in the Ohio wilderness, they celebrated with a special ration of whiskey the first victory of the US Army.

FROM FALLEN TIMBERS TO FORT GREENEVILLE

A mile and a half ahead of the Americans' camp, the Union Jack flew above formidable Fort Miamis. Within its fosse, abatises, and 20ft-high wooden walls, Campbell had 14 guns and about 400 men, reduced by an influenza outbreak to an effective garrison of 150. The British major, who had received no orders on how to respond to an American approach, knew only that he would neither surrender Fort Miamis nor commence a war with the United States. His safest course of action, he concluded, was to close the fort's gates and await an attack.

When the fleeing Indians reached the fort, they sought refuge within its walls. To their astonishment, Campbell's soldiers refused to allow them to enter. Cursing the British, they then fled down the Maumee to join their women and children at the mouth of Swan Creek. "Had the Indians been admitted," Burns recalled, "nothing would have prevented Wayne from storming the fort." The American commander instead used Fort Miamis to demonstrate to the Indians that the British would not fight his army. On August 21, Kentucky horsemen scoured the surrounding area for miles, burning trading posts, villages, and cornfields. On August 22, Wayne and his aides rode to Fort Miamis. As flames appeared from the 13 buildings of McKee's nearby trading post, the Americans began walking their horses slowly around the stronghold. As Campbell's infuriated garrison watched from a few yards away, Wayne and his aides pointed out to one another the fort's notable features. Then they departed, leaving Fort Miamis in the center of a smoking wasteland.

When Wayne returned to the American camp, he found a courier waiting with another report from Thomas Butler. On August 1, thousands of armed settlers had assembled near Pittsburgh. After some had raised a new flag to

Note: Gridlines are shown at intervals of 270yds

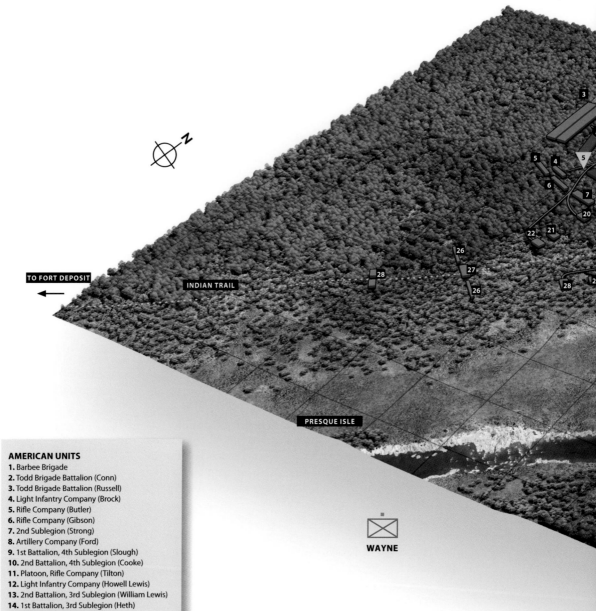

TO FORT DEPOSIT

INDIAN TRAIL

PRESQUE ISLE

WAYNE

AMERICAN UNITS

1. Barbee Brigade
2. Todd Brigade Battalion (Conn)
3. Todd Brigade Battalion (Russell)
4. Light Infantry Company (Brock)
5. Rifle Company (Butler)
6. Rifle Company (Gibson)
7. 2nd Sublegion (Strong)
8. Artillery Company (Ford)
9. 1st Battalion, 4th Sublegion (Slough)
10. 2nd Battalion, 4th Sublegion (Cooke)
11. Platoon, Rifle Company (Tilton)
12. Light Infantry Company (Howell Lewis)
13. 2nd Battalion, 3rd Sublegion (William Lewis)
14. 1st Battalion, 3rd Sublegion (Heth)
15. Artillery Company (Pope)
16. 1st Sublegion (Peters)
17. Light Infantry Company (Gaines)
18. Rifle Company (Springer)
19. Rifle Company (Sparks)
20. Sorrell Horse Dragoon Troop (Van Rensselaer)
21. Artillery Company (Porter)
22. Bay Horse Dragoon Troop (Covington)
23. Black Horse Dragoon Troop (Miscampbell)
24. Artillery Company (Massey)
25. Gray Horse Dragoon Troop (Webb)
26. Platoon, Rifle Company (Preston)
27. Light Infantry Company (Bradley)
28. Rear Infantry Guard Platoons (Reed)
29. Scout Company (Kibbey)

▼ EVENTS

1. Sparks's rifle company advances and confirms that no Indians are in the floodplain.

2. MisCampbell's dragoon troop, followed by Webb's dragoon troop, attack Indian left flank.

3. Springer's rifle company and Gaines's light infantry company join attack on Indian left flank.

4. Conn's and Russell's battalions push Canadians and Wyandots on Indian right flank back.

5. Van Rensselaer's dragoon troop, followed by Covington's troop, Brock's light infantry company, and Gibson's and Butler's rifle companies, attack Indian right flank.

6. Regular infantrymen advance in bayonet charge.

7. Indian retreat collapses into disorder and becomes a rout.

8. Barbee's brigade moves through thick woods to attack behind Indian right flank.

9. Americans pursue Indians to site of Indian warriors' camp.

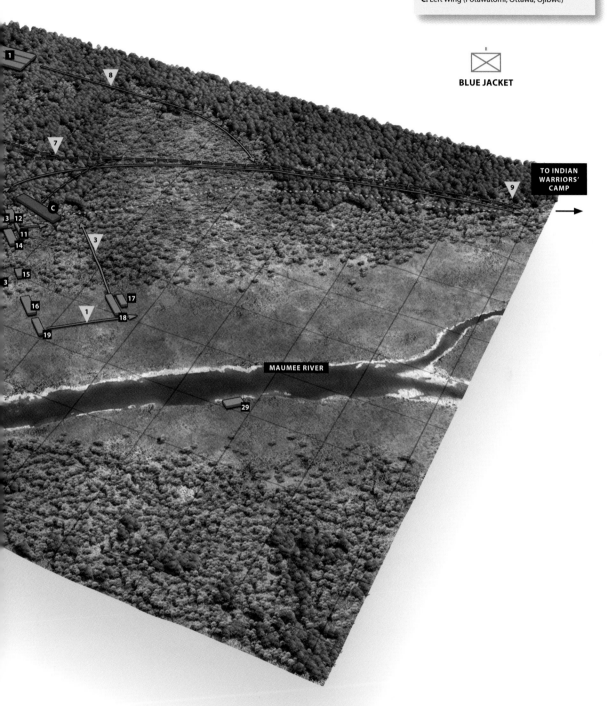

BLUE JACKET

TO INDIAN WARRIORS' CAMP

MAUMEE RIVER

THE AMERICAN COUNTERATTACK

Between approximately 10.30 and 11.00am the Americans counterattack and rout the Indians

replace the stars and stripes of the United States, others had threatened to burn the town. By announcing that Fort Fayette's guns would fire on any rebels who came within range, Butler had saved Pittsburgh. The rebels, however, now controlled most of western Pennsylvania. Led by David Bradford, a Washington lawyer inspired by Genêt, some were demanding a second American Revolution, while others were calling for western independence.

Wayne had a more pressing problem. His army's food supply was rapidly dwindling. On August 23, the Americans began marching back to the Glaize. On August 25, as the army moved toward its 23rd camp, Wayne ordered Price's horsemen to circle back to ambush any following Indians. At the site of the army's 20th camp, they killed one and wounded two. On August 27, the Americans reached Fort Defiance. There, at their 24th camp, they would remain on half rations, awaiting food supplies. On August 28, Wayne dispatched a report of his victory to Knox. On the same day, Wilkinson wrote to his friend Senator John Brown of Kentucky, and on the next to "friends in Philadelphia." Because of Wayne's incompetence, Wilkinson reported, only good fortune had saved the army from destruction. His detailed account of Wayne's blunders, he suggested, should be published, perhaps as the work of an anonymous officer.

The news that sped down Wayne's Trace, however, was of a great American victory. In Cincinnati, Ezra Ferris recalled, there "was almost frantic joy." As celebrations spread from the Ohio River to the Atlantic, the newspapers found no room for Wilkinson's criticisms of his triumphant commander. While the Americans waited at their 24th camp, each day brought them closer to starvation. The Indians, moreover, remained a constant menace. On August 30, they killed three men who ventured beyond the American camp. On September 10, they killed three soldiers and captured three civilians a mile north of Fort Greeneville. That day, however, a convoy arrived at the Glaize with the flour and oxen Wayne needed to continue the campaign. On September 14, he led his army up the Maumee, leaving Hunt and a garrison of 200 at Fort Defiance. After passing through their 25th through 27th camps, the Americans reached Kekionga on September 17. There, at the army's 28th camp, Wayne would build the second of his permanent forts on the Maumee. Although Fallen Timbers had not ended the Indians' ability to continue raiding, it had left them shocked and demoralized. On September 27, Simcoe arrived on the Maumee to find about 2,000 gathered in camps on Swan Creek. Three days later, Joseph Brant and 97 Mohawk warriors appeared, ready to fight the Americans.

Simcoe persuaded the Indians to move to Brownstown, the village of the adopted Wyandot Adam Brown, where they could more easily be supplied with food. There, from October 11 through 14, Simcoe, McKee, and Brant tried to restore Indian morale. Campbell, Simcoe told the Indians, had misunderstood his orders. The British major now had specific instructions to fire on the Americans if they returned. The council, he said, should resume the following June, when the Indians and British could plan a new campaign against the Americans. By then, he thought, the British and Americans would at last be at war. On October 17, however, a devastating letter from Dorchester reached Simcoe as he was riding back to Newark. He had received from London, the Governor of Canada wrote, a reprimand for the provocative construction of Fort Miamis on American territory. He also had been informed that Britain would soon agree to a treaty with the Americans and surrender Detroit to them.

From September 17 through October 26, the Americans remained at the head of the Maumee. As they built what would be called Fort Wayne, they nervously calculated the rate at which they were consuming their food. Scott's horsemen rode to Fort Recovery to escort food convoys. To carry flour up Wayne's, and then Harmar's Trace, Wayne sent with them almost all of the army's remaining horses. Teams of 30 American soldiers would instead pull the wagonloads of logs cut to build Fort Wayne.

The logistical problem, however, was only temporary. The demand for food at the fort would diminish when only its garrison remained. The Americans, moreover, now controlled the main water routes from the Ohio River to Lake Erie. The following spring, they would be able to transport supplies to Fort Defiance and Fort Wayne on the Miami, Auglaize, St. Marys, and Maumee Rivers. In time, they would be able to use the Wabash as well. After building a blockhouse at the end of Hamilton's Road to the Little Wabash, Wayne planned a series of new forts that would guard the water transport routes. In 1795, he would build Forts Piqua, Loramie, and St. Marys, and also, he expected, a fort at abandoned Tawa Town. Forts St. Clair, Jefferson, Greeneville, and Recovery, which could be supplied only by land, then could be abandoned.

As the American commander conducted experiments with watercraft on the St. Marys and Maumee, men arriving with food supply convoys brought ever more alarming news from Fort Fayette. The day before Wayne's army had returned to the Glaize, Washington had ordered the western Pennsylvania rebels to disperse. If they did not, he had announced, he would lead a 13,000-man federal army across the Appalachians to restore order. Attempts to assemble Virginia, Maryland, New Jersey, and Pennsylvania militiamen to form Washington's army then had caused riots in which two men had been killed. Three hundred Maryland militiamen had mutinied in Hagerstown. Eight hundred loyal militiamen from Baltimore had regained control of the town and arrested 150 men.

After escorting large food supply convoys to Fort Wayne, Scott and his horsemen left for Kentucky on October 14. A week later, a courier brought welcome news from Philadelphia. The British, Jay had reported from London, would honor the western boundaries established in the Treaty of Paris. They would surrender to the Americans Forts Miamis and Detroit, and also Forts Niagara and Mackinac. On October 27, the American commander left Hamtramck and a garrison of about 300 at Fort Wayne. His army then

This 1791 portrait by Jean Laurent Mosnier depicts Lt. Col. John Graves Simcoe in the uniform of a Queen's Ranger. (Courtesy of the Toronto Public Library)

LEFT
This well from Fort Wayne survives in Old Fort Park in Fort Wayne, Ind. (Photograph by Dale Benington)

RIGHT
Isaac Zane and his wife, Tarhe's daughter Myeerah, named their eldest son Ebeneezer after Isaac's brother, who had founded Wheeling in 1769. Ebeneezer Zane's cabin survives in his father's Wyandot village, now Zanesfield, Ohio. (Author's photograph)

marched down Harmar's Trace to Girty's Town, stopping at its 29th through 32nd camps. The Americans then followed Hartshorne's Road to their 33rd camp. On November 2 they reached Fort Greeneville, where a 15-gun salute and round of three cheers from the assembled garrison greeted them.

After sending Wilkinson back to his exile at Fort Jefferson, Wayne continued to investigate the conspiracy his subordinate had led. On November 22, Capt. Daniel Bradley arrived at Fort Greeneville with an unexpected source of information. Newman, who had returned to the United States, had been arrested. He had thought, Newman told Wayne, that the conspirators' goal was merely to prolong the war, so that the army's contractors would continue to profit. In Upper Canada, however, he had talked with Matthew Elliott and Maj. Edward Littlehales, Simcoe's military secretary. The object of the conspiracy, he had learned from them, was to detach the area west of the Appalachians from the United States. By the time Wayne's army reached the Maumee, they had been told, it would be led by Wilkinson.

As winter set in, the American commander learned that he would not need to dispatch any of his soldiers to Fort Fayette. The day before his army had returned to Fort Greeneville, Col. Henry Lee, whose son Robert E. Lee would exceed his father's fame, had led the Maryland and Virginia militiamen of Washington's federal army into western Pennsylvania. What would be remembered as the Whiskey Rebellion then had collapsed without bloodshed. Bradford and almost 2,000 rebels had fled down the Ohio toward Spanish Louisiana. There also would be no war with the Spanish or Iroquois. Unwilling to fight the Americans without British allies, the Spanish had offered to commence negotiations on American use of the Mississippi River. After the 400 Iroquois returned to their villages from the Maumee, moreover, the Iroquois and Americans had resolved their differences in the Treaty of Canandaigua.

As snow covered the Ohio woods, bitter memories of 1794 lingered in Indian camps and hunting lodges. Around their fires, the Indians talked of what had happened at Fort Recovery and Fallen Timbers, and at Fort Miamis and Brownstown. In December, Tarhe sent his son-in-law, the adopted Wyandot Isaac Zane, to inform Wayne that, whatever course the other Indians chose, the Wyandots wanted peace. In January, Indians began to appear at Fort Defiance and Fort Wayne, returning captives as a sign of good faith.

On February 7, 1795, Blue Jacket and Buckongahelas arrived at Fort Greeneville with a delegation of Shawnee and Delaware. They promised to

88

return for a peace council in July. On February 17, however, Indians killed three men and wounded four in an attack on a convoy advancing from Fort St. Clair. The Shawnee chief Pucksekaw then led 70 warriors on an extended raiding expedition. In March, at Symmes Creek, they lost one in a fight with five American scouts. On May 14, at Reeves's Crossing on Paint Creek, and May 15, at Ohio Brush Creek, they battled a party of 40 men from Massie's Station. Despite the attacks, Wayne prepared for the peace council. Pickering, who had succeeded Knox as Secretary of War, sent him instructions on acceptable treaty terms. Hunt, at Fort Defiance, and Hamtramck, at Fort Wayne, provided reports on the Indians who planned to attend.

To defeat the Indians at Fallen Timbers, the American commander had surmounted obstacles unimagined at the time of his appointment. With his instructions on treaty terms, Pickering sent to Wayne yet another letter marked "Private and Confidential." "The president," Pickering wrote on April 15, "has seen all your letters disclosing the conspiracy that was calculated to destroy you and your army, and perhaps to dismember the United States. Your success against the Indians … Mr. Jay's mission … and the suppression of the insurrection in Pennsylvania have defeated the plan."

As the time for the council approached, soldiers from Fort Greeneville prepared the ground across Greenville Creek where the Indians would camp. As some built council houses in which Indian leaders could confer, others determined directions and distances from the fort's guns. Their targets prepared, Wayne's artillerymen would be ready if the Indians attempted treachery.

Thousands of warriors might be camped at the site. Indians would be coming to Fort Greeneville, Hamtramck had reported, from as far north as Fort Mackinac. The northern Indians, who lived more than 400 miles from the Ohio River, had little interest in the boundaries of American settlement. Nonetheless, Indians visiting Fort Wayne had told Hamtramck that many northern Ojibwes and Ottawas were planning to attend the council. He had asked his visitors, Hamtramck reported to Wayne, why the northern Indians would travel so far. "It was rather a long journey," they had replied, "but from the great desire they had to see 'The Wind' (for they call you so), they would go." "I asked them," Hamtramck added, "for an explanation of your name. They told me that on the 20th of August, last, you was just like a hurricane, which drives and tears everything before it."

This reproduction of an Indian council house is in Greenville, Ohio. (Author's photograph)

AFTERMATH

"It is with infinite pleasure," Wayne wrote to Pickering on August 9, 1795, "I now inform you that a treaty of peace between the United States of America and all the late hostile tribes of Indians northwest of the Ohio was unanimously and voluntarily agreed to." There soon, moreover, would be peace. On September 6, Indians killed a man, woman, and five children at the Tush cabin east of Wheeling. Colonel Patrick Brown and 15 Kentuckians then ambushed a party of 12 Indian raiders at Blue Spring, killing 11. But on September 9, the raiding ended. Pucksekaw and his Shawnees appeared at Fort Greeneville, surrendered four prisoners they had taken, and went home.

"The war of the Revolution," William Henry Harrison would write, "continued in the western country until the peace of Greeneville, in 1795." That peace commenced a series of American diplomatic and political successes. On October 27, 1795, the Spanish agreed to open the Mississippi River to American commerce in the Treaty of San Lorenzo. On June 1, 1796, Tennessee joined the union as the 16th state. On July 11, 1796, the British surrendered Detroit. The price of peace on the Ohio River frontier, however, proved controversial. Many Americans opposed the concessions made to Britain in Jay's Treaty. Debates on its ratification in the US Senate converted the political forces that had emerged during Wayne's campaign into organized parties, the pro-treaty Federalists and the anti-treaty Democratic-Republicans. Under changing names, such parties would become a permanent feature of American political life.

The figures portrayed in Christy's *Signing of the Treaty of Greene Ville* include Tarhe, Blue Jacket, Black Hoof, Little Turtle, Buckongahelas, William Wells, Isaac Zane, Lt. Meriwether Lewis, Maj. John Mills, Wayne, Lt. William Clark, Lt. William Henry Harrison, and Capt. Henry De Butts. (Author's drawing)

Wayne lived long enough to enter Detroit in triumph. Hailed as a national hero, he spent his last months accumulating evidence to prosecute Wilkinson for treason. When he died in 1796, his treacherous subordinate succeeded him as commanding general of the US Army. In 1798, however, retiring President George Washington assumed the position.

Thousands of Americans settled within the area allowed by the Greeneville Treaty line, which ran from the mouth of the Kentucky River northeast to Fort Recovery, east to Fort Loramie and old Fort Laurens, and north along the Tuscarawas and Cuyahoga Rivers to Lake Erie. In 1800, the Northwest Territory was divided into the Ohio Territory and the Indiana Territory. In 1803, when the Ohio Territory became the 17th state, the United States purchased Louisiana, a vast region beyond the Mississippi River that included St. Louis and New Orleans. In 1804, Wayne's lieutenants Meriwether

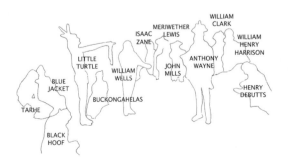

WILLIAM CLARK
MERIWETHER LEWIS
ISAAC ZANE
WILLIAM HENRY HARRISON
ANTHONY WAYNE
LITTLE TURTLE
WILLIAM WELLS
JOHN MILLS
BLUE JACKET
HENRY DEBUTTS
BUCKONGAHELAS
TARHE
BLACK HOOF

Lewis and William Clark led an exploring party through the new territory to the Pacific Ocean.

Dreams of independence from the United States persisted for a time west of the Appalachians. In 1805, thousands of Indians embraced a new religion founded by a brother of Tecumseh, the Prophet. After establishing Prophetstown, a large Indian village at the site of abandoned Fort Greeneville, they began a campaign to eliminate the chiefs who had made peace by charging them with witchcraft. At the same time, the still-scheming Wilkinson was planning with Vice President Aaron Burr, Kentucky Senator John Adair, and others to seize an area west of the Mississippi where they would establish an independent country. In 1806, Wilkinson saved himself from disaster by disclosing the plot to President Thomas Jefferson and successfully denying his own role in it.

The actions of the Prophet's Indians led them to the brink of war with the Ohio settlers. In 1808, they left Greenville Creek for a new Prophetstown in the Indiana Territory, where Wayne's aide William Henry Harrison served as governor. There, in 1811, they unsuccessfully attacked a force led by Harrison at the Battle of Tippecanoe. In 1812, the United States declared war on Britain. More than 2,000 Indians, led by Tecumseh and the Wyandot chief Roundhead, joined a British army that invaded Ohio. An American army, led by Harrison, repelled them at two sieges of Fort Meigs, a fortress across the Maumee from the site of Fallen Timbers. After an American fleet commanded by Commodore Oliver Hazard Perry captured a British fleet at the Battle of Lake Erie, Harrison led an American army into southern Ontario that included hundreds of Ohio Delaware, Shawnee, and Wyandots, led by Black Hoof and Tarhe. On October 5, 1813, Harrison's army destroyed a British and Indian army at the battle of the Thames. There Tecumseh fell and Indian dreams of reclaiming the Ohio River frontier died with him.

Howard Chandler Christy's massive 1945 *Signing of the Treaty of Greene Ville* hangs in the rotunda of the Ohio Statehouse. (Courtesy of the Ohio Statehouse Photo Archive)

THE BATTLEFIELD TODAY

Many monuments and museums mark the sites of significant locations during Wayne's campaign. A marker at 9th St. and Penn Ave. in downtown Pittsburgh commemorates the site of Fort Fayette. Monuments on Pa. Rte. 65 in Baden, Pa. mark the site of Legionville. Fort Washington, commemorated by a monument on Ludlow Street in downtown Cincinnati, is the subject of exhibits at the Cincinnati Museum Center, at 1301 Western Ave. Fort Hamilton was at the site of the Butler County Soldiers, Sailors and Pioneers Monument, a museum with exhibits on the fort, at 1 S. Monument Ave. in Hamilton, Ohio. Fort St. Clair was at Fort St. Clair State Park, near Eaton, Ohio. Fort Jefferson was at the site of Fort Jefferson State Memorial, at the intersection of Ohio Rte. 121 and County Rd. 24 in Fort Jefferson, Ohio. Fort Greeneville was in Greenville, Ohio, where the Garst Museum, at 205 N. Broadway, has extensive exhibits on the fort and Wayne's campaign.

Fort Recovery was in Fort Recovery, Ohio, where a reconstruction of the fort can be visited at the Fort Recovery State Museum. The museum, at 1 Fort Site Street, has many artifacts recovered from the battles of Wabash and Fort Recovery. Fort Adams was just to the east of where US Rte 127 crosses the St. Marys River. Fort Defiance was at Old Fort Defiance Park in Defiance, Ohio, and Fort Deposit at what is now Farnsworth Metropark in Waterville, Ohio. Fort Wayne was at Old Fort Park in Fort Wayne, Indiana.

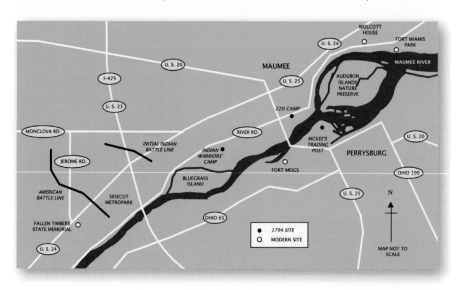

The area of Fallen Timbers today. (Author's map)

The nearby History Center, at 302 East Berry St., has extensive exhibits on the fort and Wayne's campaign. Fort Massac was at Fort Massac State Park, in Metropolis, Illinois.

The sites of Fallen Timbers and Fort Miamis, in Maumee, Ohio, are part of the as yet uncompleted Fallen Timbers Battlefield and Fort Miamis National Historic Site. The areas open to visitors are Sidecut Metropark, the scene of fighting in the floodplain on the American right flank, and Fort Miamis Park, where the earthworks of Fort Miamis remain. Fallen Timbers State Memorial, a park just southwest of the battlefield, is on Fallen Timbers Lane, accessible from US Rte 24. The Wolcott House, at 1035 River Road, built by a daughter of William Wells, displays Wells family memorabilia. Nearby Fort Meigs, on West River Road in Perrysburg, contains a reconstruction of William Henry Harrison's war of 1812 fort and a museum with exhibits on the rich military history of the area, including Fallen Timbers.

Fort Piqua was in Piqua, Ohio, where the Johnston Farm and Indian Agency, at 9845 N. Hardin Rd., has exhibits on the early Ohio Indian wars. Fort Loramie was in Fort Loramie, Ohio, where the Wilderness Trail Museum, at 37 North Main Street, can be visited. Fort St. Marys was in St. Marys, Ohio, where the Mooney Museum, at 223 S. Main St., has exhibits on the fort and early Indian wars.

Reconstructed Fort Meigs, the largest wooden fort in North America. (Courtesy of Fort Meigs)

FURTHER READING

Anyone interested in Anthony Wayne's Fallen Timbers campaign should read Alan D. Gaff's excellent *Bayonets in the Wilderness: Anthony Wayne's Legion in the Old Northwest* (2004). Other works with valuable information include the following.

Alder, Jonathan, *A History of Jonathan Alder* (2002)

Ammon, Harry, *The Genêt Mission* (1971)

Anson, Bert, *The Miami Indians* (1970)

Bauman, R. F., "Pontiac's successor: the Ottawa Au-goosh-away," *Northwest Ohio Quarterly*, Vol. 26, 8–38 (Bowling Green, Ohio, 1954)

Burton, Charles M., "General Wayne's Orderly Book," *Collections and Researches Made by the Michigan Pioneer Historical Society*, Vol. 34, 341–733 (Lansing, Mich., 1905)

Carter, Harvey Lewis, *The Life and Times of Little Turtle: First Sagamore of the Wabash* (1987)

Clark, William, "A Journal of Major-General Anthony Wayne's campaign Against the Shawnee Indians in Ohio in 1794-1795," *Mississippi Valley Historical Review*, Vol. 1, 419–44 (Urbana, Ill., 1914)

Cooke, John, "General Wayne's campaign in 1794 & 1795: Captain John Cooke's Journal," *American Historical Record*, Vol. 2, 311–16, 339–45 (Philadelphia, 1873)

Hoffman, Phillip W., *Simon Girty: Turncoat Hero* (2008).

Jacobs, James R., *The Beginnings of the United States Army* (1938)

Knopf, Richard C., "Two Journals of the Kentucky Volunteers 1793 and 1794," *The Filson Club History Quarterly*, Vol. 27, 247–81 (Louisville, Ky., 1953)

——, *Anthony Wayne: A Name in Arms* (1960)

Kohn, Richard H., *Eagle and Sword: The Federalists and the Creation of the Military Establishment in America*, 1783–1802 (1975)

Linklater, Andro, *An Artist in Treason: The Extraordinary Double Life of General James Wilkinson* (2009)

Mahon, John K., *American Militia: Decade of Decision*, 1789–1800 (1960)

Meek, Basil, "Tarhe the Crane," *Ohio Archaeological and Historical Society Quarterly*, Vol. 20, 64–73 (Columbus, Ohio, 1911)

Miller, Edward, *With Captain Edward Miller in the Wayne campaign of 1794* (1965)

Nelson, Paul D., "General Charles Scott, the Kentucky Mounted Volunteers, and the Northwest Indian Wars, 1784–1794," *Journal of the Early Republic*, Vol. 6, No. 3, 219–51 (Philadelphia, 1986)

Pratt, G. Michael, "The Battle of Fallen Timbers: An Eyewitness Perspective," *Northwest Ohio Quarterly*, Vol. 67, No. 1, 4–34 (Bowling Green, Ohio, 1995)

Simmons, David A., *The Forts of Anthony Wayne* (1997)

Smith, Dwight L., *From Greene Ville to Fallen Timbers: A Journal of the Wayne campaign* (1952)

——, "William Wells and the Indian Council of 1793," *Indiana Magazine of History*, Vol. 56, 212–25 (Indianapolis, Ind., 1960)

Sugden, John, *Blue Jacket* (2000)

Sword, Wiley, *President Washington's Indian War: the Struggle for the Old Northwest, 1790–1795* (1985)

Tanner, Helen H., *Atlas of Great Lakes Indian History* (1986)

Van Cleve, Benjamin, *Memoirs of Benjamin Van Cleve* (1922)

Weslager, Clinton A., *The Delaware Indians* (1972)

Wilkinson, James, "General James Wilkinson's Narrative of the Fallen Timbers campaign," *Mississippi Valley Historical Review*, Vol. 16, 81–90 (Urbana, Ill., 1929)

Winkler, John F., *Wabash 1791: St. Clair's Defeat* (2011)

INDEX

References to illustrations are shown in **bold**.